To My [?]

Forever.

Love you!

— [signature]

6/2017

Bravely She Flies

Bravely She Flies

Genena Woodson Armstrong

Tracy Baumer

Cheryl Butcher

Angela Cheng

Adrianne Court Petruska

Malaina Davis

KayCee Gregory

Marie Kiana

Calia Kimball

Rhonda Nichols

Frances Robinson

Amberly Simpson

L.I. Tibbets

Dawn Thompson

Cover Illustration by Mars Chosnek

Bravely She Flies

Contents

Inspired by the many stories of resilience, Bravely She Flies was born. Giving women an opportunity to voice and share their stories in their own words and in their own time. Penning personal and real resiliency experiences as a public form of expression to acknowledge, appreciate, forgive and learn while sharing and connecting. It is our dream to inspire others to join us in a movement and to bravely become authors of their own chapters in many more Bravely She Flies to come.

Transfiguration

And the day came
that I finally woke up
and realized I had outgrown the cocoon
and my wings had been patiently waiting for
me to grow into them
and so now I fly…

~Audra Erwin
The "High on Life" Coach
 www.audraerwin.com
 www.dailyinspiredmusings.com

1

"Put That Fork Down And Eat That Chicken With Your Hands"

Genena Woodson Armstrong

Dedicated to my mother, Vera Lee Jones

What's in a name? Were you given your name by your parents based on a relative? A movie character? A bible verse? Or maybe you were named after a vehicle, and your parents thought it would be cute and "different" not giving thought to one day you'd have to apply for employment and complete an application using "said" name.

Maybe you've thought about your name a million times, or maybe never at all.

I've had several names in my life: Genena, Gigi, and Nena. And several last names for that matter: McDaniel, Woodson and now Armstrong. When I think of the names given me, they each have meaning. Meaning in such a deep and profound way that I hadn't discovered until I spent time reflecting upon my life. I am a 46-year-old wife, mother, daughter, sister, girlfriend, professional business and life coach, and exhorter to the wounded. I am a 25 year HR Executive, and have spent most of my life attending educational institutions, acquiring certifications and climbing the corporate ladder. My story is one of resilience and tenacity.

When I was asked to contribute to this project, I had several emotions. I was elated and honored. Then sad. Then frustrated. Then exhausted. Then focused. Then purposed. Why did I experience all of this in one given moment you might ask. Well, when you're asked to relive painful, yet profound experiences in your life it feels almost like giving birth.

Resiliency. Specifically *"Psychological resilience."* Wikipedia defines as an individual's ability to successfully adapt to life tasks in the face of social disadvantage or highly adverse conditions. Adversity and stress can come in the shape of family or relationship problems, health problems, or workplace and financial worries, among others. Resilience is one's ability to bounce back from a negative experience with "competent functioning". Resilience is not a rare ability; in reality, it is found in the average individual and it can be learned and developed by virtually anyone. Resilience should be considered a process, rather than a trait to be had. It is a process of individuation through a structured system with gradual discovery of personal and unique abilities.

Allow my mind to wander. Wander to my childhood. My house is a small three bedroom, one bath ranch style home on the south side of Chicago. All the houses on the city block are the same. Just different colors. I am number eight of 10 children. We all share bedrooms and even the same bed. My mom and dad are married, but something just doesn't feel right. I'm not secure, even though I have food, plenty of people around me and a roof over my head. My mother is not home. Neither is my father. But I have many sisters who take care of me. Comb my hair. Prepare meals for me. One day my mom and dad fight. My dad is arrested. He's gone. My mom is crying. I am scared. And then it happens. Divorce.

There's just three of us kids at home. I'm the oldest. I remember being about 9 years old. The other siblings are grown and gone. The three of us and mommy still in the same house, but it's cold. Its winter, and we have no heat. We use hot plates to boil water to bath, and take turns in the same water. We all sleep in the same room, in the same bed, in my mother's bed because the space heater keeps us warm. We have food. People bring us food. Neighbors and people I don't know. My older sisters and brothers take us to their apartments for the weekend and that is happiness. Happiness because I know we will have food and fun, and she loves us. Back at home we have clothes to wear. It's not that we don't. It's just that we wash once a week and wear the same clothes on the same day of the week. We don't have a telephone either. When I want to call my daddy I must sneak to the pay phone on the corner a block away to call him. I tell him I love him, and to come and get us. He sometimes comes to pick us up on the weekend, and sometimes he doesn't. I can still remember and feel the roaches that crawled on me at night while asleep. They had a nest in the headboard post of the bed I shared with my little sister.

I know in my heart that this is not my life. I don't understand why my life is different from the people I see on television. The only other family that lives this way is the family on "Little House on the Prairie." But they all seem happy with their circumstance. They seem grateful. Why am I not happy and grateful? I know my life is supposed to be better. I can feel it in my soul. I sense that my little brother and sister are not fully content with the way things are for us, but they seem to be handling life much better than I. Maybe because they are younger, and are better at being content? I don't know…I just knew I had to find a way. A different way.

My mother sings to Jesus. She says "Lord" a lot. Every day. She sings and sweeps the floor. Who is He? Why is she singing to him? She seems content and at peace. How is this? Why doesn't she go out and get a job? I thought she used to have a job. Oh. She worked at a barbeque pit. That's right. When I was younger. She would bring home left overs that customers didn't buy. Why doesn't she go back there? She tells us she doesn't want to leave us at home by ourselves, and that she wants to stay home and make hot meals and be home when we get home from school so we don't get into trouble. In my childlike mind, I think "I'd rather have new clothes like my friends at school."

Then I wonder, why does my mom only have an 8th grade education? My dad graduated high school and went to the military. My sisters and brothers have jobs? And they work and they have kids at home?

"How do I get out of here? How can I live a better life for myself or my future kids? I need a plan…"

I'm 13 years old now. I can work. Or at least that's what the City of Chicago says. The city has a Mayor's summer program for inner city youth. I make $235 every two weeks. I'm rich! I can buy clothes for school, and pay for things I need! All of a sudden I feel more secure. That feeling I had in earlier days when I was younger and my dad was home and my siblings were home—that insecurity I no longer feel. I have money and I can take care of myself!

My mind is still wandering, and I'm 15 years old now. I'm in high school, and I'm working after school. I work in a hair salon where I make cash money and I'm told I don't have to report what I earn. I work illegally because I should have a cosmetology license in order to put relaxers and color onto client's heads. The stylist hide me in the back when the corporate people come to audit. I pretend I'm a client. All I care about is that I'm really rich now. And I get my hair done for FREE. My grades are pretty good, and my mom doesn't have to worry about taking care of me. She just has to care for my younger brother and sister. My older sisters are concerned that I will get pregnant, so they put me on birth control. I don't mind. I don't want to get pregnant either. I just want to go to college, get a good job and make money. I want security. That's what I want to feel. The rush of doing it myself. Taking care of myself.

Boys. Men. They're a little scary at first. I had a crush on an older man. He reminded me of *Prince*. He rode a motor cycle down my street. My heart raced. I told my sister and she said "Hmpf." I waved when I saw him at the neighborhood park. One day he stopped and said "I know your secret. When you turn 18 we'll talk." I about peed in my pants. I didn't know what to say. What secret did he know? That I had a crush on him? He was the pool life guard. I was 15. I had 3 more years to wait for him. I started hanging out at the pool more often. I didn't know how to swim. One day he invited me to take a ride with him. We went to his mom's house and I drank my first wine cooler. I was a little drunk. He kissed me. I liked it but I didn't. The next time we kissed and he humped on me really hard. It hurt. It was not fun. But he was *Prince* and he smelled good. The next time, and the time after that he took me to his brother's house. This time he entered me. It hurt really bad. There was blood. I was so scared. I called my sister from the pay phone. She called my other sister. They were mad. They picked him up and took him for a ride in the back seat of my sister's car. They threatened his life. He was nine years older than I was. This was considered statutory rape. He was never to see me again. And I was off to Planned Parenthood. No pregnancy. But lots of birth control.

I finished high school, and was accepted into college. I was the first of my siblings to attend college and graduate; a first-generation college graduate. The entire four and half years I worked really hard. I had very little money and used the Pell Grant, scholarships and loans to pay for room and board. My mother didn't want me to go off to college. She didn't understand why I didn't want to stay home, work and help her "finish raising my little brother and sister." "What good is more schooling?" she asked. It was my older sister's mother-in-law who took me shopping and bought my first sheet set for my dorm room. I had very little food or supplies so I had to learn from the other kids in the dorm what was needed in order to get started. I figured out where to get my books, what books I needed, and I hitched rides home during the holidays from classmates.

After I left for college, I no longer had a room at my mom's house. After I left, the room was used for something else. I was welcome to stay during breaks, but I knew I needed to finish school so I could pay for my own place. "You can do it Gigi. Just finish school." I motivated myself, and my sisters were proud of me. My brother would yell when I asked him for a ride to school but he drove me anyway. He always thought one of my boyfriends should be driving me to school. They all loved me, but weren't much help when it came to navigating university life. They taught me all they knew. And I love and appreciate each of them to this day for all they instilled in me.

Want to know something else? I never visited the dentist growing up. My father pulled our teeth when they were loose. I had several cavities. Whenever the cavity got really bad I would just switch sides and chew on the teeth that weren't rotten. The front ones were fine. It was the molars that had cavities. One day in college one of my molars had a hole and it cracked on the inside—on the inside near my tongue. It scratched my tongue when I talked. It scratch my tongue when I swallowed. I couldn't concentrate I was in so much pain. I cried. I called my best friend Michelle and she called her mom who had a friend of the family who was a dentist. "Would he do her a favor and take care of my teeth?" is what she asked him. I was a poor college student. I went home for the weekend and he pulled my tooth. He didn't fill and crown it. He pulled it. I thanked him because I didn't have to walk around with a scratchy tongue and pain, but I had no teeth in the back. That molar is still missing today.

As I mentioned I finished college in 4.5 years. That half of a year was spent my freshman year taking Reading and study skills classes. I never told anybody this but I got a 12 on the ACT. Not once, but twice when I took it the second time! I never tested well. I was considered an above average student, but because I went to school in the Chicago Public School system, we never learned to study. Not blaming the school system, but I sort of am. I passed that first semester with all A's, and began the Spring semester with the rest of the college kids.

I majored in Business, with a Human Resources focus. I have always been good at building relationships. I knew whatever I majored in it would have to involve "people." I also knew I had to major in a subject that would ensure a job upon graduation. I pledged a sorority (Alpha Kappa Alpha Sorority, Inc.) and I was an RA (Resident Assistant). I interned all four summers of college, and I managed to graduate and get through without getting pregnant. That was a major accomplishment for me and my family. That doesn't mean I didn't manage to have multiple boyfriends at one time. It was back then that I realized that I used men. I can't say it was just for entertainment. I did fall in love once, but our timing was off. I was 3 months from graduation and had plans that did not include him. Security. Every bad situation I faced, 'security" was often my motivation. Resiliency. It took resiliency at every turn of my life it seemed to get through and keep going. But I'll get back to the men in my life a little later…

Back to my college career--because of my internships during the summer (money I used to pay for school) I landed a job prior to graduation. That was very unusual for a girl from the south side of Chicago in 1992. A lot of my friends were forced to work Retail until they found an "office" job. I'll never forget. I was offered $28,000/year. It happened! That feeling…I was once again secure. Neither of my parents ever made that much money. I had broken the cycle of poverty.

So I got a job, now the question was where would I live. I couldn't go back home. Not only was the distance to my job from my mother's house too far to commute, but I had become very independent and couldn't imagine living with my mother. All those memories of childhood haunted me.

It was my big sister in Gurnee, Illinois who took me in. She was married at the time with 3 kids and had a large enough home that I could stay in the guest room until I saved enough to get my own apartment. It took me one month before I signed my first lease. I also bought my first car and had enough money to eat. Hallelujah! I was on my way.

Back to the men in my life...I can't remember how it started. The "multiple men" syndrome that is. I just remember after losing my virginity, I had my choice of men. One of my big sister's told me "you need a different man for different reasons." So I continued to see the motorcycle guy, but I also had a "college" guy. Then I had a guy that made me laugh. A guy who had a job. And then a guy I actually had fun with. I never seemed to find one guy who had it all. One day my mom says to me "Gigi just choose one!" So I did. I chose the man who is now the father of my two boys. He and I married. I was 25 years old. He was 29 years old. We had two beautiful boys because that is all he ever wanted, and all his mom said she would fund towards college.

I appeared to have it all: marriage, children, career, church and a handful of friends. Sure, my marriage was okay, my career was going okay, my kids were healthy, but why wasn't I happy? Why did I have a tendency to seek out pleasure elsewhere? Men had become a "sport" to me. They were only used for my purposes and pleasure. Of course, they got pleasure from being in my company, but I was always in "control." As long as I can remember, I taught myself that I didn't need a man. I could take care of myself. I tolerated men to get what I wanted. A ride to school, a date, flowers, then eventually children and the image of what society said I was supposed to have. I didn't hate men, I just didn't have a whole lot of respect for them, I guess. Sure, I loved being around them. I enjoyed intimacy with them. I liked being treated pretty, and enjoyed receiving gifts and being picked up for dates. I even got those butterflies in my stomach when I really liked a guy. I cried over a guy once or twice, and even pursued a guy that wanted to end our relationship. I just didn't understand my relationship to men, and how this shaped the woman I had become.

My husband and I ended our marriage after 16 years. It was a very sad departure. He did not want to end the marriage, but at the same time he didn't enjoy being married to the "me" I was turning into. Which was different from the me he married. I didn't want the marriage to end, but also felt very oppressed and untrue to myself. I felt like I had been following a script for a play that somebody else had written. I knew that in order for me to become the best "me" I had to go my separate way. My children were young, and I knew that it didn't matter the age of the child; divorce was hard at any age. I had to start anew, and so I took my 41-year-old self and filed for divorce. I asked the Lord to forgive me, and show me the path to peace within.

The next 5 years would be tumultuous. The journey to finding oneself is never easy.

In many ways I was like Julia Roberts in *"Run Away Bride."* I tried all the different ways you can cook an egg to see which way I liked my eggs best. In the midst of "tasting eggs" i.e. trying out different types of men, I was also an unemployed single mom. I lived in a 2900 square ft house, with a mortgage and bills. I would be unemployed for exactly a year before I found another job. I used all of my savings, my 401K and sold my designer handbags and gold to make ends meet. I cried often, and I dated often. Some of the guys were losers, some became friends. I dated police offers, ex-cons, executives and pro-athletes. Chefs and men with gold teeth. Short and tall. Black, white and Hispanic. Like I said...I tried all the ways to cook an egg. I even considered asking my husband to come back. I knew that was totally unfair to him, and would not bring myself to use or hurt him in any way. I was at a low point in my life. I never considered suicide, but I often thought about running away.

Running away from myself is what I was doing. Running away from reality. Running away from doing the hard work of digging deep inside to pull out the real me. Who and where did I draw my strength? What job or career path did I really want? What did I want out of the rest of my life? What did I really believe from a faith standpoint? Who are the types of people I want to surround myself with? I wanted to be proud of myself. I wanted my boys to be proud of me. I wanted to live life abundantly—like the Bible said in John 10:10 when Jesus said "The thief comes only to steal and kill and destroy. I came that they may have life and have it more abundantly." I also wanted to be remembered for being a great woman of God. Someone who would be remembered for what she did for others.

Well I dug deep. I cleaned out that "gook" in my soul I didn't even know I had. Yes I saw a therapist. Yes I talked to my girlfriends—old and young. Married and single. Christians and those that I never would have guessed cared about me. Neighbors and those that knew me from when I was Gigi from 95th and Green. I spent time at home with my mother. I visited my Nana in Georgia. I listened to praise and worship music and CD's from famous ministers. I lit candles. I fasted. I cut off relationships. I made new ones. I changed the way I used to think. I learned success was not about failing; but that success was failing and then getting back up. Success is about being RESILIENT. It's not the end, it's the journey.

I wish I could give you a package with a bow and say "This is what I did to overcome the challenges in life." You could just "oooo and ahhhh" and open it up, and magically everything would be better in one instant. I wish I could tell you I figured it all out after one terrible occurrence in life. I wish I could tell you that my mother-in-law didn't know what the heck she was talking about when she said "You just keep on living." I wish I could tell you which kinds of people to avoid. Which ones to trust and that you should only associate with certain people.

But I will tell you is this:

My mother told me when I was 14 years old "Always be yourself." I'll never forget this incident when I was 14 years old. I was eating fried chicken with a knife and fork at a fancy banquet she and I were attending. It was an awards banquet that I was invited to for having good grades. My 8th grade teacher picked my mom up and drove us to the event. I remember being at this fancy table and I remember copying the way my teacher ate her chicken. My mother leaned over to me and said "Girl put that fork down and eat that chicken like you always do." I put my fork down and picked up my chicken with my fingers. And when I did this, my teacher followed and did the same thing! I'll never forget that day. It is engrained in my head for life. I learned from that day this: Because I chose to be myself, I gave permission for my teacher to be herself. Therefore others to be themselves.

So I end my writing with this: Be the you that God created you to be. He uniquely fashioned you in your mother's womb. Psalms 139:13-14 NIV says "For You created my inner most being; you knit me together in my mother's womb. I praise you because I am fearfully and wonderfully made; your works are wonderful, I know that full well."

In 2014 I remarried. I married a man. Not just any man, but a great man. He looks at me and sees my internal beauty just as deeply as my external beauty. He allows me to be myself. He loves me for all of me. He loves all the names that make up who I am. He loves Gigi, Genena, Nena and of course Mrs. Armstrong. He is a man that I full well know God used to help me realize I can trust God through a man—through my husband. I no longer look for security in

money, and even in men. I find security in who I am in
Christ Jesus. I am me. And I am resilient.

Genena's Resiliency Lessons:
1. Be true to yourself.
2. Don't be afraid to go the road no one else has
   traveled.
3. Cry when you need to. Then dry your tears.
4. Keep a circle of people around you who accept you
   for who you are.
5. "Trust in the Lord with all your heart. Lean not on
   your own understanding. In all your ways
   acknowledge Him, and He will direct your path."
   Proverbs 3: 5-6.

Genena Woodson Armstrong leads the Coaching and Women's Ministry for Proclaiming the Word Ministries. Genena's passion for hope and healing for women of all ages stems from her upbringing. Born and raised on the south side of Chicago, by a single mom with 9 siblings Genena understands and has lived a life "abase and abound." Her authentic love for people, and her engaging and authentic personality is what initially draws those around her. Quickly what Genena will share it is the light of the Lord within that fuels what people see in her, and how God chooses to heal and grow people through her.

Genena is a wife, mother and ICF trained Executive and Life Coach. She brings over 25 years of Human Resources experience. Her education, certifications and experience speak for themselves. Currently Genena is an Executive

Coach and Human Resources Consultant working with individuals and companies on a contract and interim basis. Coaching is simply her lifelong calling, and God given gift.

Armstrong's prior experiences include Vice President & Executive Recruiter with The Jacob Group, Director, Diversity and Inclusion at CHRISTUS Health, Vice President of Diversity and Inclusion for Wells Fargo Bank, and the Target Corporation as Executive Recruiter for the Marshall Field's Company. Prior to Target, Genena held many human resources roles within Pillsbury and Siemens Corporation, where she served as Human Resources Generalist, College Recruiting Manager and Diversity Strategist--developing and implementing a wide range of human resource strategies and initiatives.

Genena holds a Bachelor's Degree in Business Administration from Illinois State University and completed graduate work at the University of Minnesota in Human Resources and Industrial Relations. She is a certified Senior Professional of Human Resources (SPHR) through the HRCI, and a Certified Diversity Management (CDM) recipient from the Institute for Diversity, American Hospital Association Division. Genena is a former board and executive committee member of CIS/Communities in Schools. Genena's professional organization memberships include the National Association of African Americans in Human Resources, the National Association of Health Service Executives, and Alpha Kappa Alpha Sorority, Inc.

Genena is also the contributing author of "Breaking Barriers: A Woman's Toolkit for Success" published by PWN.

She is married to Rev. Leroy R. Armstrong, Jr., Lead Servant of Proclaiming the Word Ministries and Teaching Pastor of First Baptist Church, McKinney, Texas. They have one adult daughter, Olivia (Boston, MA) and two sons, Carter "CJ" (17 years old) and Jamison (14 years old), and an orange Tabby "Simba."

2

Facing Addiction: Learning the Healing Power of Compassion

Frances Robinson

Resilience has been present throughout my life in many ways. As a small child, my Grandfather first taught me about it. I have the great joy of being named after my Grandfather – Francis - who I remember as a tall, graceful, and unyielding individual. He could recite Longfellow's poetry from his time in grade school and silence any of his fifty grandchildren with one look from his hypnotizing stormy eyes. When I was about ten, I distinctly remember tears running down my cheeks while I was taking a walk with him along the lane of my childhood home. I ran one hand through the tall grass and the other clutched his tightly. I confessed to him the great weight I felt of shame and embarrassment because of an incident earlier that day. He found the perfect response saying, "there is never any reason to feel embarrassment. Embarrassment means you are so arrogant as to believe that you are perfect." My Grandfather had multiple, similar aphorisms that all emphasized the important balance of humility and self-acceptance and often a reframing. He always encouraged me to step back and take on a new perspective. We bonded over many, similar walks and he always emphasized the importance of loving myself through moments of imperfection and to seek out progress rather than focusing on the mistake.

The most challenging events have been my greatest teachers and the lesson my Grandfather tried to instill as a child carried over into my young adulthood. Between the ages of 18 and 25, there are two events that stand out as particular crossroad. During college, I recovered from an eating disorder and then after graduation, I began building a relationship with a recovering addict. These two journeys challenged me differently, but each was equally as powerful in fostering my own understanding of resilience. I was often lost and forgot the aphorisms my Grandfather so carefully instilled, but once I could reframe the situation and build a new perspective, then I was better able to find my way.

I would not claim that most 18 to 21-year olds are generally the most self-aware individuals, and I was no exception. During this time, I spent so much time thinking about me that I lost any ability to clearly perceive myself and my actions. Beginning fall of my freshman year, I was training for a dance audition and fell prey to classic societal and artistic pressures of the "ideal" body type. Predictably, I was hiding food, skipping meals and obsessively weighing and calorie counting. What began as an innocent 'get-in-shape' tactic quickly deteriorated into a lack of self-worth and an eating disorder.

I distinctly remember attending dinner at the house of a long-time family friend. They were kind and generous. I imagine they sensed my insecurities and often invited me over to share their good food, welcoming space, and endless amounts of love. That winter evening, I felt accomplished because I had not eaten all day. I was anxious not to ruin such an excellent day and I managed to move the food around my plate expertly to make the plate look emptier. Out of politeness, ignoring my biological needs, I limited myself to just three tiny bites of everything. At the end of dinner, they offered me dessert in the form of a glazed, baked apple stuffed with honey and cinnamon and all things delicious. My sickness convinced me this was a test, and they were offering me the heavenly apple simply to judge my weight and my mental fortitude to resist the temptation. I declined, but they insisted on wrapping it and sending it home with me. Back in my dorm room, I set it on my desk and engaged in a staring contest with an inanimate object. I was starving. Finally, I hungrily devoured all of it and promptly felt overwhelmed by a familiar feeling of shame and guilt. I was so angry and embarrassed with myself. I had been so disciplined all day – how could I ruin it with such a thoughtless action. I began to panic and cry. Unable to control the tirade of negative emotions, I ran to the bathroom to purge myself of the devilish calories. Throughout the disorder, I struggled to balance a consistent feeling of shame, anxiety, and self-hatred. In public, I was convinced everyone was staring at me – judging me for being too fat or disgusted that I would dare eat. I used to stare at myself in the mirror for hours and mark down on my body or in a notebook everything that was wrong about myself. If I went home, my mother and father would push food toward me and stare at me with concerned eyes. I told myself they were being unreasonable. Unable to cope with the tirade of constant fear and self-loathing, I became an expert at isolation because facing the judgement of the public eye was overwhelming. I avoided going home, going out with friends, and even going to class. Much of my time was spent blaming other people for my self-loathing and unhappiness. *They* were too judgmental. *They* did not eat healthy enough. *They* were not inclusive.

This mindset and actions continued for a year until one day my mother broke down in tears in front of me. I suddenly realized how much pain I was causing her and I committed myself to trying to eat normally, but the emotional struggle of the eating disorder stayed with me through the second year. Even when I began to try and eat routine meals – I had forgotten how to eat. I no longer knew what a normal portion looked like, or what was appropriate, healthy food. When I felt like I had overeaten, I would work out obsessively. I stilled weighed myself excessively, avoided mirrors, and felt shame and humiliation on days when I had gained any weight at all. By the end of the second year I was exhausted, afraid of people, afraid of myself and in complete emotional shambles. Over spring break, during my Junior year of college, I called my brother at about one in the morning and sobbed and told him everything. Every thought, emotion, fear, and struggle that was demonizing my mind. He, of course, called my parents and we all agreed it was time to seek therapeutic help.

It took me two more years to fully admit to my inner struggle and the first step was the recognition that someone I loved deeply was being hurt by actions I honestly believed were only directed at myself. It never occurred to me that someone else may be impacted until my mother confronted me. Upon reflection, months of therapy, and learning to seek gratitude in times of struggle, I have come to the conclusion that my bulimia was driven by selfishness. I was so convinced that *my* happiness and *my* success was dependent on the superficial way *I* looked that I stopped thinking about anyone else. I was wholly obsessed with my own emotions that I stopped offering emotional support or service to anyone else. Only myself, my weight and my eating habits mattered for two, full years. When I reached out to someone, in this case my family, then this flicker of selflessness saved me. By hurting myself I demonstrated an inability for self-love and an immense narcissism. The world had become all about me. I was living in such fear of other people's judgement of *me* that my egoism prevented me from loving myself as well as others. I have talked to other individuals who have suffered from eating disorders and there is a fascinating commonality. For those of us lucky enough to recover in a healthy manner, the turning point was often the realization that we were hurting others with our actions. I admitted to myself that I had a problem after witnessing the pain it was causing my family. In many ways, I had forgotten the lessons of my namesake, my Grandfather, who had pushed for self-love and acceptance. By looking beyond my own experience and changing my perception of the world around me, I could begin to heal.

The second turning point for my recovery arrived when my therapist gave me an assignment to keep a Thanksgiving journal: each day I wrote down a bullet pointed list of items for which I was grateful. The journal changed my perspective of myself and this life because I began to view the world not from a perspective of what I am missing but instead to a perspective of what I was so lucky to have. I changed my habit of thinking from a consistently negative mindset to a more habitual positive outlook. I still use a daily gratefulness journal and I especially use it when I am having a particularly bad day. It changes my perception to focus on what *I have* as opposed to what *I don't have*. Similar to my Grandfather's original advice, I reframed my thinking and accepted my imperfections. The Thanksgiving journal became a tool from which to build greater resilience.

I learned resilience from my eating disorder and from my own process of recovery. The Thanksgiving journal and the eating disorder taught me to look beyond myself. When I realized that my mother was hurting because of my actions, it was a selfless moment of clarity, and serves as a reminder that in my darkest moments, there is healing power in reaching out to others. I am most resilient and healthy when I can experience a hardship and respond with profound love and service to other individuals. When I pretend that I am the only person in this world that matters, then I allow arrogance and self-deprecation to overshadow the immense power of caring for others and holistically living from a space of humility, gratitude, and love. For me, resilience is a mindset of choosing to see the best in a situation and to demonstrate compassion toward oneself and others, even on our hardest days.

My Grandfather's advice held true for my eating disorder even if I did not see it at the time. Reframing and looking for spaces to grow is my own bedrock for resilience and this became especially important as I worked on building a healthy relationship with myself in addition to others. About six months before graduating with my undergraduate degree,

I fell in love with a wonderful man and our relationship underlined the lessons of resiliency I had fostered from childhood.

We originally met each other half a world away conducting ecological research projects on soils and indigenous plants in Kenya. We shared many experiences: going on Safari, staying up late listening to the rain as we shared our love for Sir David Attenborough, and optimistically brainstorming ways to make the world a better place. Both still undergraduates at the time, he was a brilliant engineer with a quick sense of humor, an unending reservoir for kindness, and strong love for Trivial Pursuit. We were perfect for each other. Amongst his many beautiful identities, he was also a recovering addict.

We first started dating while he was still actively using his drug of choice: Alcohol. Halfway through our first year together, I became a painful witness to the destruction and despair that addiction can have on an individual and a family. One standard night with friends, he disappeared after a night of gallivanting and it was not until the next afternoon that we would find him in jail. For two long years, I watched as he battled the enormous fees and insatiable needs of the criminal justice system while maintaining his relationships and report at school.. It is a miracle of his own resilience that he maintained straight A's with a double major and held down a job while juggling the seven-mile bike ride in the humid Midwest summer and struggling with emotional burdens such as the shame of explaining to his advising faculty why, on house arrest, he was unable to take the trip to their research site. The same desire to cope with negative emotions by obsessively controlling my eating was similar to the need to escape reality through alcohol. My therapist pointed out that my eating disorder is its own type of addiction. The feelings of shame and humiliation I felt about myself before helped me empathize with his own shame and humiliation that came from facing the societal stigma that surrounds addiction. Afraid to face his school friends should they judge him, he isolated himself in his apartment. He sunk into a deep depression and I was terrified he was suicidal. For a naive and hopeful young woman, it felt as if the world was crashing inward and suffocating me. Our relationship and my relationship with my community and family suffered as he and I fell I deeper into an isolating place of depression and codependence that eventually led to our break up.

We both needed to step away and gain perspective. I felt shame for somehow failing at a relationship and failing to stand by someone suffering so badly. Yet, my Grandfather's words, this time, stayed with me. I actually wrote them on my mirror to see them every day as a reminder that mistakes and imperfection were opportunities for growth. Some part of me knew the relationship was not over and we both sought out programs to work toward our own healing and recovery. I began attending Al-Anon meetings and he attended AA meetings. One of the main tenets of the programs is to find ways to be of service. Still living in the same city, and keeping a healthy relationship as supportive friends, we began volunteering together at community organizations such as the Farmer's market and the local Humane society. We each committed to making our communities, our work, and our families a priority. It was through this selfless service that we began to repair our emotional health and our relationship. After about eight months apart, we reunited, and two years later we are now engaged. We are currently pursing graduate degrees in different states and we started a tradition that each evening before bed, we practice the lessons of my eating disorder by sharing three things for which we are grateful. We learned from the lessons of our first break up and our separate struggles that keeping our communities and families as a priority is a promise of resilience and self-care. Together, we seek out volunteer opportunities or small actions to be of service to someone on a single day. The ups and downs of our relationship taught me that resilience is not just one thing, one day. It is a process of patiently working toward a selfless, grateful, and thoughtful existence. At my most recent Al-Anon meeting we discussed one of the program's tenets: "Participation is the key to harmony." The concept of participation is an excellent reminder that hiding from life's challenges will not solve them. Nor is it necessary to face challenges head on before I am prepared. By actively seeking ways to aid people from a place of love, then I can build the community support and the mental fortitude to move forward. By committing to gratitude and service, he has not touched his drug of choice since November 2013 and has become a shining example of what healthy and committed recovery can look like.

We continue to revel in our imperfections. I still have bad days when I look in the mirror and think I should skip lunch. He still has isolating moments when he thinks about picking up a drink. However, resilience is using the lessons my Grandfather first taught me as a small child and stepping away from this moment. I can reframe my own thinking because when I think I am not good enough or skinny enough, then I am operating from an attitude of deficit. Instead, the entire day changes when I take action through gratitude or service to see the world from an asset-based perspective. Resilience is not perfection. It is instead, the awareness of my own imperfection and the recognition of my immense power to grow from an experience. My early twenties were profound times of growth in which the experiences of recovering from an eating disorder and then navigating challenges of a unique relationship taught me powerful lessons about resilience. In my own summation: life's twists and turns are adeptly navigated with gratitude and selflessness. First, I can change perspective to better understand others and remind myself that I'm not the only person in this world that matters. Second, I can act through service. My fiancé and I will be married later this year in 2017 but as a graduate student on the West Coast, I live with two other Ph.D. students. I can take simple acts of service by making my housemates breakfast or offering to give someone a ride or sending my fiancé an unexpected gift. I am armed with the knowledge that I can tackle most of life's problems when I consciously accept and love my imperfections and then choose to act from a space of generosity, compassion, and love.

Discussions of self-love and humility were the first roots of resiliency that I would continuously turn to as an adult. To my Grandfather's original point, there is clarity in a change of attitude, a new framework, or a change of perception. It is, even in the miniscule moments of life, that I began to understand the power I have when I choose to change the way I see a situation. My childhood experiences, lovingly fostered and shaped by my family is eloquently explained in a recent article by Maria Konnikova[1] who explores the strength perception has to foster resilience. When I can love myself with my imperfections rather than blush or self-deprecate each time I make a mistake, then I am progressing toward the best version of myself. This is underlined by Konnikova's pointed question: "Do you conceptualize an event as traumatic, or as an opportunity to learn and grow?" This is a poignant question proving that how I perceive a situation is more important than the situation itself. I can choose to laugh at spilling coffee or I can choose to grumble and add it to my list of frustrating incidents for the day. Unfortunately, it is often simplest to frame a difficult situation from an egocentric perspective and obsess about how it is impacting *me* in a negative manner. Without reframing, this mindset is too rigid and inflexible to offer resilient outcomes. My conviction of my own perfection can barricade me from correcting and learning from my mistakes. Instead, at ten years old, I steeped in resentment and shame until my Grandfather reframed the incident for

---

[1] Konnikova, Maria. (2016). *How People Learn To Become Resilient*. The New Yorker. 11 February 2016.
<http://www.newyorker.com/science/maria-konnikova/the-secret-formula-for-resilience>

me. I become a resilient individual when I can step outside of my own head. By perceiving a challenging event differently, it no longer holds me captive. Instead, I can forego irritation or sadness and move forward. I can choose to perceive an event as a teacher and one that makes me stronger, more compassionate, more giving.

I still think often about walking hand in hand with Grandfather with the sun on my face and his warm hand guiding my small and tearful self along the gravel lane. He taught me my first lesson in resilience. The bumps along the way, as I learned about myself and learned to build a life with someone else, only fortified his kind words that remind me to reframe my life perspective with great humility and self-acceptance.

A native of Central Indiana, Frannie grew up with five goofy and mischievous siblings and two very normal and patient parents. She received her B.A. in Biology from Indiana University and then slowly made her way across the U.S. to Washington state. While there, she explored the beauty and glory of the Puget Sound by frolicking with ferns and making friends with goats. She is currently pursuing an M.Sc. from the University of California where she studies everything from food to politics to culture and identity. Frannie is an RYT-200 certified yoga teacher and enjoys procrastinating from school work by brainstorming creative ways to go on long-distance "dates" with her fiancé who lives in Wisconsin, going running, taking dance classes, and wandering around the beautiful mountains of California.

3

The Ivory Tower Dream Becomes the Nightmare That Awakens Me

Cheryl Butcher

I had the opportunity to "retire" from a corporate high pressure computer career in 1992. The company for which I was working was closing its marketing office in West Lafayette, Indiana. I jumped at the opportunity because I was well aware that I was rapidly reaching the top of my technical technology curve and the downhill ride was not going to be pretty.

My husband was a tenured professor at our local university so the option to relocate wasn't a very good one. Plus I had grown up in this area and I was very comfortable living in the rural community with big cities only a couple of hours away in several directions. Of course, I could have opted to take a new role in any of those big cities. I could have opted to face the long commute on a daily basis or rent an apartment during the week and just come home on the weekends, but that wasn't the life style that I wanted to live.

I knew that I had been under a lot of corporate stress to perform. I was always putting myself in situations where I was the "expert," even though the day before I didn't have a clue about what new expertise I was going to need to use. I thought it was a major accomplishment if I could understand what problem a customer was having in enough detail to relay it to someone at a support site and then to be able to get back to the customer with the answer that would solve their problem. On a really good day, as the customer was describing their issue, they would solve their own problem just by talking through it! It was such a relief to be able to solve their problem just by listening to them talk through the problem logically.

After I "retired", it took me 3 months just to be able to meet a friend for lunch without having a nervous meltdown. The thought of having to be somewhere at a specific time was just too stressful! That was when I knew I could never go back to the corporate rat race and had to find a different path. The stress was just too much and my self-confidence level was too low. At this point in my life, I felt I needed to have all of the answers and learning that I didn't really have to be the "expert" in everything was a long, hard lesson for me.

After much thought and searching, I decided that I would go back to college and get my Master's degree. My husband was supportive of my decision and since he was already on the academic schedule, it would make our lives easier since our "busy seasons" would be very similar. I applied to enroll in the Instructional Design and Educational Computing curriculum which was a good fit with my technical and professional skills. My undergraduate college experience wasn't typical so I felt that I needed to have a more normal experience and really enjoy the life of a student even though it was as a "mature" student.

My last college experience wasn't the normal route. When I graduated from high school back in the 60's, the Vietnam War was going strong. My high school sweetheart was drafted. One thing led to another and let's just say that we were married in September and our daughter was born in March at Ft. Carson, Colorado!

Our marriage didn't last long after he returned from Vietnam. He was definitely not ready to settle down and accept being a husband let alone a father. It didn't help that back then, I was perfectly content to be a wife and mother and had no desire to enter the working world. Coming from a farm background, I believed then that my job was taking care of the home front! We were much too young and it simply didn't work out!

As a young single mother, I went to work as an accounts payable clerk. Working full-time during the week and sometimes a part-time job on the weekends didn't leave me much free time. Luckily, I had a colleague and friend encourage me to apply for a scholarship to attend college on a part-time basis. She even volunteered to watch my daughter while I was taking night classes. I was fortunate enough to receive the scholarship and started taking 6 hours of coursework a semester. If I had taken another class, I would have been charged full fees and that wasn't an option!

Being awarded the scholarship was huge. Not only did the money help greatly but having a group of women believe in me and think I was worthy of receiving their scholarship was priceless. It was then that I realized how much having someone believe in you meant and I vowed that I would return this gift to other women who were struggling to make a life. Now I am an active supporter in two local non-for-profit organizations that assist women in getting their lives on track after they have experienced homelessness or an abusive relationship. I am very pleased to be able to give other women a chance to make something of their lives and I only see that part of my life expanding into other areas of support. I truly believe that it is extremely important for me to mentor young women who are struggling in their life and careers because I know how important it can be as they strive to make a better life for their families.

If you do the math, you'll have figured out that it definitely took me more than 4 years to complete college. Thirteen years after starting, I received my bachelor's degree in management from Purdue University! Hallelujah! I was so happy and proud that I had persevered and accomplished my dream to be a college graduate. I was now able to fulfill my dream of working in corporate America.

After leaving that very stressful corporate job, I decided that I deserved a more normal college experience so I enrolled in a Master's program in a field that fit my skills. Since I was very proficient in technology, loved to teach, and really loved to learn, Educational Computing and Instructional Design matched perfectly. With my job in corporate America, I had been a systems engineer which was a very technical position. I also had the opportunity to teach clients how to use this new technology which meant I was always learning something new so that I could teach it! Since I was a mature student in my mid-40's with a lot of business experience, I was asked to manage the rest of the department's teaching assistants and I also co-taught several classes with different professors in the department as well.

I thoroughly loved being in education so when I completed my requirements for my Master's degree, I just kept right on going for a PhD.

I had to have several discussions with myself because I always thought someone with a PhD was super smart and I surely didn't put myself in that category! I worked more closely with many professors with their PhDs. They were smart and very well-educated but not necessarily Einsteins! So I was able to make peace with becoming a PhD – or at least I thought I had.

I enjoyed learning, teaching and conducting research but I didn't like writing research papers. You would come up with your question for your hypothesis, conduct research and gather data which was challenging and very enjoyable. The part I didn't like was using someone else's research to explain and validate my project. You really couldn't come up with too many conclusions that someone else hadn't already found. There were some minor points but nothing significant – at least to my way of thinking. And usually what you did discover was not very earth shattering but really just plain common sense. Needless to say in a world of "publish or perish", I was going to perish.

I completed all of the course requirements for my PhD and finally completed writing my dissertation. But to my utter shock, I didn't pass my dissertation defense! Maybe I really never did internally accept being a PhD and being addressed as Dr. Butcher after all.

During the PhD process, I had read several other dissertations and it was common knowledge that there had not been a candidate in several years that hadn't passed their dissertation defense in my area of study. Usually there were a few corrections that needed to be made or some additions to a section or two in their paper. But they had passed and only needed to make a few changes to receive their PhD. So you can imagine my shock and disappointment when I didn't pass. I had always been a good student receiving mostly A's and B's throughout my entire education experience so this was devastating to me! How could I have failed? What I had anticipated as a joyful accomplishment had just turned in to my worst nightmare!

As part of the defense process, all of my committee members had plenty of time to read my dissertation and let my major professor know if they had any concerns about my work. So not only was I blind-sided but my well-respected major professor was perplexed as well. The wind was knocked out of my sails and I had no idea what to do next or where to turn. It was NOT a happy day.

I had always completed what I had started so I couldn't imagine not completing my PhD. What would I do now? How could I face my loved ones? It took me a long time to "wrap my arms" around not receiving a PhD and it was extremely difficult to tell my friends and family that this dream had come to an abrupt end. Talk about baring my soul – it was one of the hardest things that I had ever had to face. I didn't handle failure well. I was definitely not seeing any positive from this experience only the devastation.

I was a part-time adjunct professor for two different educational facilities while I was writing my dissertation, so I continued teaching for no other reason than as a distraction. It was easy and at this point in my life I really couldn't handle anything else.

Deep in my heart, I knew that academia was not where I wanted to stay. But I wanted that choice to be my decision not someone else's. How could I have allowed this to happen and now what was I going to do? How was I going to be able to overcome this disappointment? What direction was life going to take me now? I thought I was in control of my destiny and tried to control everything. Now I was rudderless.

After much soul searching, I finally decided on a career in real estate. It offered a flexible schedule and allowed me to make a reasonable income. I was aware that after having such a flexible schedule for so many years there was no way that I could go back to a 9 to 5 routine. I couldn't put myself in the stress of corporate America again. I didn't think I could survive that much stress again without having major health issues. It wasn't the number of hours that was the issue, it was the idea that I had to be so rigid in my routine. It would also allow me to remain where I was physically and not require that I relocate. It seemed like a good idea so I pursued that option and became a licensed real estate agent.

My first year as an agent was extremely difficult. I had trouble reaching out to friends to let them know I was now a Realtor. When I was expecting to have received my PhD and be called Dr., being called a Realtor seemed to be a big step down in the career chain. But the more I admitted to myself that I wasn't going to be a Dr. and that was OK, the easier it became to call myself a Realtor. When you are making your life in commission sales, it is a requirement that friends and family know what you are doing so that they can refer their friends and colleagues to you. So not being able to admit to my failure was a double negative!

I was lucky enough to have found another agent in my office who had a similar experience in academia as she too was an "all but dissertation" grad student. It helped me greatly knowing that I wasn't the only one who had experienced this unexpected and unfair ending to graduate school and had chosen a career in real estate. Isn't it interesting how synchronicity happens?

Over the next several years, I have come to realize that all of my prior work and education experiences gave me the knowledge and the tools I needed to become a successful Realtor. As my career has developed, I am not only a successful agent but have also taken on leadership roles at the local, regional, state, and national levels. I am also teaching pre-licensing classes to those who want to become real estate agents. And recently, I was given the opportunity to become the Managing Broker for one of the major franchise offices in our area. I truly enjoy mentoring agents and helping them grow both professionally and personally. Life has a way of coming full circle!

I could never have planned this career path more than 45 years ago. No way could I have predicted how each career I had was going to get me where I am today. But I have learned and have always believed that when one door closes another one opens. Even though neither the shutting of the one door nor the opening of another may be what you wanted at the time but it is often what life gives you. If you learn to persevere and keep on going with a positive can-do attitude, life will turn out better than you could have ever imagined!

Life is a constant crossroads and I still am working daily to improve and enhance the life I am so blessed to be living. It was after my husband passed away that I was once again reminded of my opportunities to open new doors. For my 65th birthday, my daughter gave me a ticket to a Tony Robbins event entitled "Unleash the Power Within". I knew that attending the event would be life changing but I had NO idea of how much. I had been a casual follower of Tony for several years and had a copy of one his very early audio tape (yes, audio tape) but had never taken it farther than just listening to them occasionally. At the event I learned that once you become a "firewalker" you realize you can do anything that you set your mind to! You are free to choose your own path and there are plenty of resources available to you if you are just open to them as they appear in your life.

I now know and believe that you can change your attitude in the snap of a finger, thoughts become things, and that we live in abundance. Every minute you have the choice of whether you want to have a positive or negative attitude. If you perceive an event as negative, it will be --- but, if you can see the positive in the same event, it can turn out to be an awesome learning experience. I'm not saying to be a Pollyanna but to look for the good in everything that occurs. It will make a drastic difference in your life.

If you adopt the attitude of the "Little Engine that Could" and just keep thinking that you can, one day you will realize not only that you could but that you DID!

Resiliency lessons that I have learned are ---

Adopt a "can do" positive attitude. What have you got to lose? I can guarantee that you have a lot to gain from this simple act.

See every event as a positive. Even if it at first appears as a negative, look for what lessons you can learn from this experience. There is always a "silver lining", sometimes it just takes a lot of searching to find it!

Don't try to control what happens. Go with the flow. The only thing you can control is how you perceive an experience. You can't control what others do or think so just don't try. It will make your life so much easier just to accept and go from there.

We are here to become the best "us" we can be, so just keep learning and changing. A Native American belief is that the bigger the spirit that is trying to be born, the greater the troubles that it must overcome. In other words, if the door is closed find another way to get to where you are going – either over, under, around or make another door or window to get through. It is your choice – just keep reaching for your goals!

Cheryl is life-long resident of the Lafayette, Indiana community. She was raised on a farm by loving, hardworking parents and had the Midwestern work ethic instilled in her.

She is fortunate to be a mother and grandmother and thoroughly enjoys spending time with her family. Between her daughter and granddaughter who live in Dallas and her grandson who is currently living with her, they are constantly challenging her to try new things and adventures which keep her spirit young. She loves to read, travel and is just generally curious about the world she lives in. Being a life-long learner, she is always trying to figure out the "whys" of everything she can.

Her career has included being a Director of Computer Services for a local CPA firm, a Systems Engineer for IBM, a technical consultant for local schools and businesses, adjunct faculty at Purdue University and IVY Tech Community College and a Realtor. Currently, she is the managing broker of RE/MAX Ability Plus in Lafayette.

She is very involved in local charities especially those that assist women in their struggles to lead an independent, rewarding life. She is a teacher and mentor and willingly shares her expertise as often as possible.

Being recently widowed and searching for the meaning of life, Cheryl started her spiritual journey after attending two Tony Robbins events. Having attended other workshops and reading several top authorities in the area of spiritual growth, she is enjoying her journey and anxiously looking forward to what the future has in store for her. She has recently purchased an old Victorian home and knows that it will be playing an important role in her life for the next several years – maybe as a writers retreat!

4

Wounded Heart, Healing Faith

Ms. KayCee Gregory

I believe a little background will add clarity to my story, the journey of almost 5 decades. The religious and politically conservative city in the southwest area of Texas where I grew up, and currently live, is progressive in terms of attractive for business development and growth, maintains an average cost of living, and is considered to be a great place to live, work, and raise a family. The people have a deep sense of pride in our heritage and the majority who live here were also born here. There is a high level of sophistication in the arts, education, and opportunities available here. We have kept up with the changing times while maintaining our legacy and identity as a major city. I hope I will be able to give you enough "visuals" with my words that will take you along on my journey, then to now. However, none of us can rewrite history as much as we might desperately want to do. Experiences really are our own personal "history" that we have lived out; the following represents a significant amount of mine.

A beautiful, sunny day in October was dawning and I couldn't wait for it was a day I had looked forward to for a very long time! I was getting remarried to Trent, a man I believed was the love of my life! We knew each other for over three years and had dated exclusively for much of that time. Surely we must have known everything worth knowing about each other after all that time, right? Everyone had a little bit of anxiety when they were taking such a big, life-changing step, right? Why should I be worried, it was just me feeling anxious, I was no different than everyone else in the same position, right? That's right, I shouldn't be! I had been divorced for 5 years, an adult and

54

was so convinced I had set out on the plan God had for my life. Time had come for me to get us dressed and ready to meet the rest of my family in the chapel of our long-time church home!

Some importance in shaping me into who I am today lies in understanding a little about my first marriage and life leading up to / after it. After my divorce from John, I felt completely alone and so very broken. We had the perfect lives for the 6 years we were married. Perfect in the sense that we never argued about anything. I was only16 years old when we married having graduated high school early and he was a 20 year-old college sophomore who dreamed to be an airline pilot. I longed to be an industrial psychologist who was driven to be spiritually and intellectually passionate about helping / serving others. I'm not sure I truly knew more at this point in my life, but I did know I felt woefully inadequate somehow, deeply searching for life's purpose; a feeling inside of much more to do.

We came from hard working, successful families. We were very close to both sets of our parents and spent a lot of time with both. My own parents were entrepreneurs and they entertained every weekend most of my growing up years. By 10 years old, I could manage most elements for a successful dinner party, and I was driving by myself at 12. My relationships were always with adults.

It was not unusual to find heavy drinkers and smokers in those times and ultimately it deteriorated the health on both sides of our families albeit rejected by both of us in terms of lifestyle. But it also meant we were more and more heavily involved in being caregivers. John and I believed that men should definitely be the head of household and to make the final decisions should we ever disagree. We were simply too young to understand what that thinking meant spiritually. John should be the spiritual head of our household yet he wasn't equipped to be, nor did he really have the desire to be. I realized this gap too late. During the late 1960s / early 1970s women had very few, if any, opportunities to have careers as we understand today. Many of us had the burning desire without support from anywhere else.

God took us a direction other than that of the airline pilot family. John discovered he had blood pressure higher than could be allowed as a pilot, so that door permanently slammed shut. We were hugely disappointed. John redirected his attention to learning to instruct helicopter pilots and that became our immediate direction. I threw myself into supporting him, our families who now had serious health issues within them, and to making our home a beautiful haven of serenity. John and I would fight about me going to college which I desperately wanted to do, but would not pursue if it was only my dream and not ours as a couple, and certainly not if it was against God's plan. We would discuss my drive to do more with my life, but neither of our families understood it, nor did John. As a result, I really had to accept that this was a decision, a choice, I had made, and found as many creative ways to grow as possible. Nothing I did, however, could remove feelings of being inadequate.

56

I went to work for a major telecommunications company and settled into a routine way of life. It was then we began to discuss having children. We both loved kids and believed we would be good parents. Our plans had been all along that I would work until our first child was born, and then stay home to raise however many we were blessed to have. The path we would travel took 5 long years of fertility tests, therapy, etc.

Finally, our daughter was born and our life as a family would soon be over. Literally 8 months from her birth, John had decided the day our child was born that he could not be married anymore. He ran from any form of responsibility and so did his family. My own father was critically ill with a terminal disease leaving my mother no strength to help me nor me her. I was no longer within the safety of my own home and everything I truly loved; I had no education, no job, no money, no place to turn, never balanced a bank statement, and had never been isolated. While I had always served others to a fault, I could rest when I wanted to and when I needed to; I was fearless because God had answered every prayer; now the world was full of darkness for me, and with another mouth to feed.

No matter how many tears I shed or kept inside, no matter how many times I begged John to change his mind, there was a huge secret he had been running from. He had kept it from me until a few months after our daughter was born; John was gay. I could understand cognitively, but my heart just couldn't grasp it all. I felt betrayed in every fiber of my being. All the dreams we had, plans gone. All the unanswered questions about why his sexual drive was lower than mine, lower than those in professional advisory roles would suggest it should be, now seemed much, much clearer. I had no frame of reference leading up to this shocking news, however, and was definitely too shy to ever have wanted to discuss openly with anyone. My reality wasn't changed, I had an awful lot now to do, and it could never again only include me I had a daughter too. I had to find a job, an apartment, a loving daycare environment, and a much more economical way of doing things. I loved John, but I feared what people would say. For many years, no one knew what had happened between us, or what had caused the divorce. It took an awful long time, lots of work, to get past it. There were no examples, no models for me to see; while there had to have been others, no one was talking. I got more and more independent as a result of no one to turn to.

After I took care of the immediate changing demands, a routine was established and I could catch my breath. No, the tears did not go away, they just stayed inside for "another day". There was not a moment when something was not demanded from me, of me. But I looked around at the many women I worked with (in health care), truly beautiful, passionate people, and I was reminded of my fear of ending my life without fulfilling purpose, true meaning; feelings of this is all there is meaning simply routine, mechanical movements and that life was missing. My life was so isolated I felt what I had experienced was shameful, and I was desperately lonely. I was as involved as I possibly could be in my church, but did not find room there for single women somehow. I continued to ask God all the wrong

58

questions: Why me for this misery? What did He want to teach me? Why had I not learned it by now? I was never anywhere other than work, or with my daughter. I had a fear of damaging her by seeing me date lots of different men, so I hid behind her due to my own heartache. At least for the moment, it worked to keep me going; it did not take away my desire to go to college, however, and to find some level of stability, acceptance. I had developed a deep desire to create a much different life for her so that she could grow up knowing she would go to college, and could be anything she wanted to be. In the mid-1970s society was just beginning to understand equality has got to be for everyone. In many ways, she was my vision of a better tomorrow, the reason failing was not an option, my sense of survivor instinct so that she would have a better tomorrow with choices I just didn't have.

At the daycare, there was a wonderful woman, Mrs. Jones. She took pity on me and would babysit for almost nothing when I had to take on a second job, and then a third. Without child support and making just above minimum wage, there weren't many options for us. I absolutely had to find a way to make a better future for us. I believed the path to a better future would have to include education although no one in my family had ever gone to college. I may not know what I did want, but I knew what I didn't and that was a deadly boring life with no contributions to make things better than I found them. I began to ask others I ran into how they had afforded going to college. Ultimately, I received an educational grant that allowed me to begin my dream of attending college and my life, our lives, changed forever. The job I got when we divorced was in accounting at a major hospital. I decided that must mean I should be an accountant rather than an industrial psychologist and it was the academic path I took. While I struggled having not had the proper foundational knowledge, I made up for it in hard work and persistence. I found I truly loved to learn and the growth I began to see in myself would sustain me through many of the dark days I would face in the future. My decision making criteria was faulty, I am creative and a much better fit within the world of marketing; however, an accounting degree opened the door for me to work for a major airline which began a truly rewarding career for me spanning more than 2 decades.

Soon after I started to college, and while working in the hospital, I finally let a new man into my heart. Trent was sophisticated, bright, and seemingly confident. By the time we met, he was an executive and I was a hard-working, driven single mom, just attending college. Being divorced for 3 years at that point, I had figured out a lot of life. Trent and I talked a lot about what education meant to me personally, and he already had a degree putting us on common ground. Trent shared joint custody of his own son. In addition, he was involved in the Big Brothers organizations, and I was a Big Sister. We attended the same church, and as possible, he would babysit as I was a student 4 nights each week, every week, for 4 years in addition to the full time leadership position I maintained. We made time for each other, and I was happy.

I was able to survive quite well with very little sleep, and still continued to manage all life stresses by myself. I wanted to be sure that our relationship could be almost isolated with no outside influence, or demands beyond our children or each other. It created a very false sense of reality, unfortunately. I was admired for all the things I could do, and it never occurred to me to expect anything in return or that I would ultimately hit a snag somewhere such as exhaustion. I trusted he would help me if I needed it, and he assumed I would never need it for I had let him believe only he was important. He wasn't perfect, but I believed he was real, and I loved him deeply. We made plans so I could complete my undergrad degree after we married. There was no doubt we were already a very close family unit of 4.

Our honeymoon was the beginning of the arrival of stress, and violence. After a couple of days, I wanted to call to check on our children who were staying with close friends. During the call to his ex-wife, Mary Jane, we discovered she had taken a job in another state and would be leaving in less than two weeks and she was taking Trent's son. There had been little over-reactions to stress while Trent and I had known each other and he had every right to be upset with this news. What I did not see coming was the violence that would ensue, and the underlying anger from unsettled trauma during Trent's much younger years that would bubble up in just about every area of our lives. What this really did was begin a tragic life of mostly isolation for me. Domestic violence has never been acceptable; it has only recently become something absolutely not tolerated.

Literally generations have dealt with these situations often in silent endurance and humiliation because the blame has been placed on the woman leaving no avenues for escape. Since I had never experienced this behavior with Trent, I somehow deeply believed it would, somehow, resolve itself. I had received several promotions at the hospital and my career progressed as my academic accomplishments grew. Unfortunately, I couldn't make enough money to support us and go to school, too, so I sought promotion in a division office for a leading paint and drywall manufacturer not far from where we lived so that my earning potential could continue to grow along with my career.

Mary Jane moved with their son without telling us how to locate them, causing us worry beyond all proportions. Trent became almost a recluse. He became sullen and typically non-communicative. Wouldn't everyone be upset was what I thought. I developed a pattern of waiting to study when everyone else was in bed and no one needed anything from me. I cooked most meals on the weekend so there was minimal requirement from Trent as he helped take care of my daughter while I was in school practically every night.

A week after our honeymoon, Trent went on a business trip for a couple of days and I was pretty happy for the diversion it would give him. We still had no idea how to contact his son. Returning on Friday evening, I had prepared a favorite dinner we could share as a family. I could not know he was raging inside. Within moments, he had grabbed me and thrown me out of our studio apartment. I was so afraid, but tried to make sense of it as I went back inside only to be faced with more physical and verbal abuse. He raged upstairs and I crumbled to the floor. After a little while, he came down fully calm and apologetic for his behavior. He swore would not happen again and said it was because he was sick with worry about his son. I wanted to believe him, and found lots of ways to rationalize to myself how it would never happen again, and I should not be afraid. I had bruises, but nothing broken except my spirit.

The many, many bruises on my outside did not compare to what I felt on the inside. I had never seen anything like it from Trent, nor felt the sting of anyone's physical abuse. After he went to bed, I tried to make sense of what happened. I wanted to believe this was behavior that would not recur. I was still working on my degree and I sold most of my belongings when we married. It was the real beginning of living in fear that I had never known could exist, and I definitely stopped growing emotionally from that moment. I asked what had happened, but I feared the answer; I was emotionally, and financially, trapped for what would be decades. I had no complete education, no money, no furniture, no place to go, along with a broken heart and body. I worked and went to school so much when I wasn't taking care of the needs of my child, that I found myself with no one to look to even for emotional support. The driving force to getting up every day was to stand on my own again for my child and me; I had no hope for us if I did not finish my education.

I prayed nonstop. Still asking the only question I knew to ask, why me? It took me a very long time to realize I had made all the choices, and God was crying all the time as I. The more I tried to get Trent to talk about his abuse, the more he withdrew. We didn't really have any friends, and even when we did, I was too embarrassed to tell anyone what was happening behind closed doors. Not only was it still happening, it escalated. After a few months, my mother and her friend came over and I had covered up my newest bruises with long sleeves. Ultimately they saw them though, and only commented that he must have a bad temper. It was another reminder that I was on my own. It was like a silent, right-of-passage moment, in a secret women's club for me; I was determined to never allow my own daughter to live in isolation, without help, hope, and a future.

The more I learned, the more I realized what questions to ask, and the more I tried to solve the underlying causes of the domestic violence. I feared being gone to class too long for what might happen when I was gone. When home, I did not say things that I feared might cause an argument, or take a position I knew was different than Trent's. I continued to only study after everything everyone needed was done, and that was never prior to 10:00 p.m. The toll it all might have on me, or my child, just never occurred to me, or when it did, I somehow justified with the vision of a better tomorrow for both of us. Since I had no friends, family, co-workers I could talk to, the decisions I made were only made with faith and keeping my own counsel lacking any real objectivity. The decisions I made were really more out of desperation and fear for survival than anything else. I was successful academically and professionally progressing in both, but a complete failure on the personal side.

64

It is never easy to answer the causes of domestic violence. As a woman who had always been an adult taking responsibility for everything and everyone around her, I could only make excuses for how it was my fault. I was working, I was going to school, I was in debt prior to our marriage, I I I…..my daughter's father did not pay child support. While Trent's son now lived in another state, I had asked him to help me with my daughter. He had adopted her legally but it's just not the same. I was grasping at life and how to create happiness. I believed strongly we needed our own child, and Caleb was born 3 years into the abusive situation.

School was my only safe haven and I guarded it at all personal costs. While I paid a heavy price of setting myself aside in many ways, this was my life raft. It was where I could convince myself things weren't as awful as I knew they were. I could not yet see I did not deserve such cruel behavior, I had no frame of reference and lost all objectivity. I would pray and pray for The Lord to release me from this drive, the vision for a better tomorrow through education. Surely I had been wrong in His direction? And every single time someone would be used to speak to me that it was His plan, to continue. So I did ultimately completing a bachelor's, a master's and PhD within our 23 years together.

Trent's violence was always directed at me, and I wanted to believe I did everything possible to shield my children too. I continued to make decisions first, and to tell Trent later. Situations were avoided if I felt there was a chance someone would know what was happening inside our doors. Our children had friends and went to their homes, but seldom was anyone at ours for fear of what might be exposed. Caleb was in a private school which made this a little easier. Time just kept on marching by, and the violence continued to grow. I refused to stop and take the time to really look at the toll it was having on me for fear I might never quit crying, or that I would just give up. The children did not deserve lack of choices, lack of options that had been true for me. It drove me forward at absolutely all costs. A better tomorrow for them, and for me, could only come if I was strong enough to keep going.

During the days immediately after graduating with a bachelor's degree in accounting, the country was in a deep state of recession, finding a job was especially difficult. I went to work in the tax accounting office at a major airline and believed, finally, our future was set. Unfortunately, we were both in cost-contained industries, healthcare and air transportation which was about to experience heavy losses due to the recession and deregulation of the industry. I feared either or both of us being laid off so I worked harder and harder to be seen as a valuable asset, too valuable to be laid off. A life with no income literally meant disaster for me, and would mean I would never find a way out of despair for myself and my children. Working in 24/7 positions also, however, adds more strain on relationships such as ours. The more I worked and went to now graduate school, the more violent he became. And the more fearful I became, the more desperate our situation was. I would hide every chance I could, and I watched my own life pass me by. It was just less painful that way. Even the church we attended

66

was off limits for me. Trent worked for a hospital that was heavily supported through our church, and he was well known both places. Even if people knew and believed me, I felt my security would be seriously jeopardized so I kept silent even in channels that could have been open to me had I not been so afraid. They all knew the person I had known and married, not the person capable of the violence I endured.

Then Caleb was 11, Trent's other son was 19 and took a drug overdose unbeknownst to us. It was during their family grief counseling that I was told for the first time Trent's father was a domestic violence physical and verbal abuser. Things just got a whole lot clearer for me. All of the 14 or so years we had been married by then, all of the excuses I had made taking all the responsibility for the stressors as my own fault being the cause of them all, just wasn't true. Although we had been to counseling for our children many times, he had kept hidden he was reliving the life his father gave his family. Now I knew I had no hope for any better tomorrow, and it was a thought I simply could not tolerate, that of being a survivor stuck in my marriage. A master's degree completed, a career upwardly mobile through airline operations, and our children all the while paying the price emotionally as much as I had tried to convince myself they were shielded, of course they weren't. I have not said much about my daughter's development until now, only that she was a major motivator for me throughout all of those troubled years. Even before Trent and I married, she was willful, never happy, and always on an emotional roller coaster, experiencing only highs and lows with nothing in between. We went to many doctors, but it was only as an adult was she diagnosed with bipolar disorder. On March 3, 2017, she passed away of apparent accidental overdose, and after many years of prescription drug addiction. From her birth to her death, she motivated and inspired me.

I still knew, somehow, God had plans for me to complete 3 degrees and the last one was still in progress. While I had begged for release, He didn't. What He did tell me, though, was that He would use all the bad choices I had made for good if I would let Him; I would ultimately be a voice for others and that He had not brought me here to leave me here. For the next 9 years of our lives together, I clung to this reality. Caleb deserved a future with education, as a destiny. He and I studied together almost every night, a source of tremendous joy for me! I saw his growth, and it also inspired me to keep going. We shared successes, disappointments, fears, and humor!

I told Trent I would stay with him until Caleb was off to college. I slept on the floor of the office for many of those remaining years. Did it ever eliminate the violence? No. Did it minimize it? No. Was there anywhere to turn in those years? No. Did I want to believe I could fix it myself most of those years? Yes. Was it a dark and lonely journey? Yes. Is my story uncommon, unique? Unfortunately, no. As Caleb started off to another state for college, I dedicated all of my energy to finishing my doctorate lacking only the dissertation. Being in many leadership roles throughout my career, both before and at the airline, I began to see that I could only have minimal impact in shaping the thinking of new hire employees right out of college; rather the real opportunity to make a societal difference would be possible only from the classroom and for me, from within the university communities. After completing my degree, I had the God-given opportunity to transition from the airline to a small, private, religious liberal arts institution and I jumped at the chance to become a professor! From that professorial role, and after demonstrating administrative leadership strength, I progressed to the role I have today which is as the leader of a significant graduate school of business. All combined, I have been serving in the university for almost 18 glorious years.

Do I have a calling now where God has made good, over and over, His promise to turn all the bad decisions I made into divine purpose for Him? Absolutely. I'm in a place I can share some of what I've learned with others who may feel that same darkness in similar situations. I can remind them they are not alone. I can help them understand there are always options and choices, and if I can find the Light, so can they, too. Having spent over 20 years in the airline industry, I learned the art of business, and the goodness in humanity across the globe. The last 18 years in Christ-centered higher education has taught me how to ask the right questions and to be often a voice other women need to hear who may be experiencing same / similar situations or worse. I have learned how to serve with humility and deliver the awesome power of His grace. Finally, I am where I was born to be. Life is a journey every day. Given the same choices before me if I were to relive it all, I would make the same decisions, the same choices. My prayers might not be why me, but rather why not me. I would definitely choose to connect at the heart and soul with other women for a better tomorrow. I would be fearless fighting for the rights of all, and that is what I pray for all who will read about this journey. The freedom, the reward, I now feel is in giving a voice and continued strength to others. Instead of hiding behind a smile so people won't guess the pain I feel, the pain is gone and people can see if I can do it, so can they.

Resiliency Tips:
1. Do not let anyone on this earth make you fearful! In fact, you have God on your side and that means fearlessness. He equips all of us with unique gifts and talents with expectations that we are to fulfill His purpose for our lives. To all of us much has been given and much is expected. That means to fulfill His purpose, the full potential, for our lives. We are so not alike! No one has everything which would be in contradiction to all of being unique children of God. He expects us to use our talents and gifts and to have plenty of action to get to through that journey.
2. Ask for help when you need it. And watch to help others who may be in need.
3. Nurture, keep a close support group who have only your best interest at heart and you theirs. Do NOT isolate yourself, ever.
4. NEVER settle. I don't mean don't ever be satisfied, but don't settle means always be driven toward excellence in everything you do. Never, ever let anyone take your dreams from you.

5. Walk humbly with God. Pray in everything you do. You will never be perfect, accept that fact. And accept that you are plenty good enough.

6. When something doesn't feel right, it probably isn't. Don't rationalize away warnings of the heart and mind. Pray for The Lord to slam shut all the doors you don't need to walk through.

7. Truly, deeply love yourself. Allow yourself forgiveness for mistakes you make. We all make them. Mistakes may be unfortunate; mistakes don't define us. What defines us, our character, is from how we handle those mistakes, learn from them, and move forward.

8. Live a life of purpose, set your priorities to follow your life's calling, and go for it!

I will pray this chapter touches the heart of those who read it, that it is a source of peace and it is a resource for personal power. I have promised God that I will allow Him to work through me for good outcomes from many of my bad decisions. Sharing is just one of those ways.

About Kaycee

KayCee grew-up in Central Texas, entered first grade at the early age of 5, graduated high school and married at 16. She graduated from Texas Christian University in Fort Worth, Texas, with a BBA degree in Accounting after studying 4 nights per week for 4 years. Within a few years of graduation, she went to work for a major airline where she remained in a career there spanning over 20 years. KayCee, while remaining with a family & home based in Fort Worth, had the good fortune to move around frequently responding to many opportunities for advancement within the airline family. In fact, movement was encouraged and seen as a positive to build competencies, and to become a greater asset to the organization.

At the end of the first year, she began an MBA in Technology at the University of Dallas accomplishing that goal at the end of 5 years. Being driven as a lifelong learner, KayCee began pursuit of a PhD in business at the University of North Texas, a degree that would take almost 10 years to complete. At graduation, she had completed emphases in organization management, and higher education with an emphasis in college teaching. Ultimately, she returned to UNT to pursue doctoral academic qualification in marketing as well. After a career as a business leader in the airline industry, and the completion of a PhD, KayCee was prepared to pursue a second career, one within the business of education. Her career as a university professor with expertise in marketing and technology, primarily with administrative leadership responsibilities, expands nearly 18 years, and she is currently the Chair of the Graduate School of Business at a small, private religious liberal arts university. She has been recognized as the Business Faculty of the Year, and is quite passionate about serving the needs of adult business students so that they may reach their full potential, their calling. She supervises dissertation committees, and leads doctoral students in various capacities. KayCee is also an active volunteer in the DFW area honored to serve in many significant leadership roles. She lives by faith, unashamedly Christian, and is totally committed to the integration of faith and learning.

KayCee lives in Fort Worth, TX, within walking distance of her son. They are very close as a family and spend many hours together being amateur street photographers, and watching or attending college sporting events.

5

Wisdom Revealed Within The Shadows of My Heart

Adrianne Court Petruska

"Blessed is the one who finds wisdom, and the one who gets understanding, for the gain from her is better than gain from silver and her profit better than gold."
(Proverbs 3:13-14 ESV)

If I knew turning 50 was going to be this good, I would have done it much sooner. Of course, not, but there certainly are some great advantages. Instead of fumbling through much of my 20's and 30's, and even some of my 40's, driven much by fear, doubt, self-pity and selfish ignorance, I now can objectively reflect on my collective experiences with calm, humility and forgiveness. I now can thank God for the lessons learned and wisdom revealed. And, with growing older, I am learning that holding onto things that have happened in my life with anger, resentment and regret is entirely overrated. It is considerably better and healthier to accept each and every experience, no matter how painful, as gifts from God.

This is not to sound as if I am tooting my own horn or being braggadocios, but it is important to reveal a glimpse into my life now to give context into and connection with a raw and personal reflection I am exposing. Some would say I am successful, fortunate or even lucky. I have a great family with my husband, son, daughter and three furry, four-legged creatures filling our home. (Of course, we are not void of the typical dramas of two teenagers in our midst.) We live in an affluent neighborhood with great schools, drive nice cars, go to church, serve our community and go on nice vacations. I have made my way up the corporate ladder to succeed in sought-after senior executive positions. Yes, there are sacrifices as I work long hours, but in general, life is good.

Young female professionals and recent graduates regularly ask me about what are the keys to success in my career and life. Typically, I will impart some nuggets about being focused, balancing caring for your family and teams with achieving financial results, giving recognition, investing in professional development, having faith and so on. Generally, all good stuff. Each will nod and take notes and graciously act as if they have never heard such brilliant advice. If I were deeply and sincerely truthful to them and myself, while all of these things are good and important, it is the experiences collected in our lives with the resiliency with which we respond to them, and the appreciation for each we are given, that is of utmost influence and importance to our lives and careers.

When I was asked to join the mosaic of women who were each writing a chapter, I panicked. What could I possibly share? Should I picture the darker sides of my childhood with my parent's physical and emotional hostility toward each other? Could it be about my Belgian grandmother, Gigi, who was a great force in my childhood? Would I conceitedly tell about how impressively I was promoted into an executive position at a young age? Would it be of interest that I took-off with a college friend on a whim to London, not for a prestigious study abroad program, but to work minimum wage jobs? Would it be of interest to share the reasons why I was engaged three times and was dubbed the runaway bride by my friends and family? Or, it would be too fantastical to share the discovery of a painting I almost sold at a yard sale that was worth quite a sum (Franz Bischoff's *Arroyo Seco*)?

While I grappled with which one of these stories to voice, I knew there was one that I should tell. I, however, risked being exposed as a fraud. Here I was telling myself and others that turning 50 gives you grace and perspective to look back at collective life experiences as gifts with calm, humility and forgiveness, and an appreciation for wisdom gained. There was one story, if truly expressed, was splattered with self-pity, regret, anger and guilt. I was holding onto this like a baby holds on to their security blanket. Each time I was reminded about writing my chapter, I would stuff this story into the shadows. Again, and again, responding with being too busy with work and life which simply did not afford me the time to properly devote to this project. God continued to nudge me to go deeper into the shadows to reveal something greater. I finally acquiesced and listened, so here it is . . .

As I hinted earlier, my parents struggled in their relationship most of my childhood. It began with physical altercations, police involvement and intermittent separations and later it became deep and silent distain. They stayed together for financial reasons and "because of me." The day I moved out of the house for college my mom implemented her plans to pack-up and leave my father with only minimal notice.

78

There was nearly 13 years of difference in their ages, but the gap was greater than age. She was 52 and ready to reinvent herself and her life. My father was 65 and experiencing the profound effects of chain-smoking throughout most of his life. Starting as a young teenager inhaling unfiltered cigarettes and exposure to elements as a sailor in World War II caused irreparable and progressive damage to his lungs. He had frustrated brilliance. His stubbornness and intellectual arrogance mixed with his deteriorating health squashed his ambition and made him nearly unemployable. Being a night watchman with the structure and solace of the graveyard shift suited him and his circumstances well. He had no intent on reinventing himself or embracing life.

I desired to ignore my childhood, leave my parent's problems behind and move full swing into the college experience. As college friends boasted about their fathers' occupations (doctors, lawyers and businessmen - oh my), I shared the circumstances of my dad with only the closest few. I would call or visit him on obligatory holidays and I knew that he looked forward to these, but I gave them sparingly. The last thing on my college-life agenda was to sit in a smoke-filled and disheveled apartment with my father. And, because of the nearly two-generation difference in our ages, it was difficult for us to find a common language. While the guilt was slowly seeping into the deep corners of my heart for not spending more time and showing more compassion for him, I would push that away with distractions of school and young twenty-something adventures.

As I was finishing college and ready to begin my life, my father's health was dwindling rapidly as did his ability and interest to work. Simply reaching down to tie his shoes caused his lungs to gyrate into near exhaustion. After a visit with him shortly after graduating, I knew that he could not continue to live in his environment that had deteriorated into squalor. Work was becoming impossible for him with no significant financial means, other than his Social Security, to fully support himself. I recall this day and moment so vividly. I was lamenting to my mom about what we should do about him. She abruptly halted our conversation with, "he is your problem dear and not mine to solve or to worry about anymore."

And, so there I was an early twenty-something, ready to party and fly free with my new job and life. While college friends were moving to cool condos near the beautiful Southern California beaches, heading to far-off lands like Chicago and New York, and having long sleepovers with their love-interests, I was gaining a 70-year-old chain-smoking, grumpy and unkempt roommate. I did my best to ignore him as much as possible even though we were living together. Leaving early in the mornings for work, coming home late in the evenings, but he was always there just waiting, waiting and waiting. And, did I make him wait. I was angry with him and I resented him. My life was just not fair per my twenty-something values. Poor, poor me. None of my friends had their father living with them, nor did they relate or understand or care to understand. Poor, poor me.

There were flashes of understanding, connection and kind gestures between us. Generally, these were rare sightings. We continued living like this for several years. At one point and early on, we had a roommate, but mostly it was just us bound together in our living circumstances because of DNA and finances. I was burdened with college debt. The two of us sharing rent, utilities and grocery bills and I trapped with cleaning up after him constantly. My life continued and his declined into deeper isolation.

As my career grew, I could afford nicer living arrangements for us and a promotion took us to Texas. While not the exact scenario, if by any chance, you are a fan of *National Lampoon's Vacation*, my father was in many ways the Aunt Edna of my move to Texas. At the time, I joked when we were moving that I tied him to the back of my car and hauled him across multiple state lines to Texas.

After several years of sharing housing together, I could see the light at the end of the tunnel. I paid off all my debt and we made plans for my father to live on his own. We were both ready for this separation. Together, we located a senior living complex that was affordable, provided meals and easy access to maneuver his scooter around with oxygen tank in tow. Freedom at last! And, the pattern began again. I would call or visit him on obligatory holidays, take him to doctor's appointments if all other transportation alternatives were exhausted (keep in mind, this is well before Uber). I knew that he looked forward to these visits with me, but I gave my time sparingly.

Why me? Why was I the one who had this burden and not my friends? Why did my mom feel it was fair to leave this to me? Why was I guilt ridden and angry at him? Why could I not look beyond the smoke, and mess and arrogance to see an imperfect man that was more than just these things? A man that lost his mother as a young boy and was shipped off to fight in a war because there was no other place for him to go. A man that returned from that war to adopt his half-brother as his son. A man that imparted his brains to his daughter convincing her at a young age that she should have the courage to do anything, knowing that he could or would not do much with the latter part of his life. A man that grew depressed and isolated. A man that struggled to take his last breath and died alone in his disheveled room. A man that would have loved to meet his grandchildren had he cared for his health and lived longer.

So here I am filled with regret, guilt and self-pity mixed with anger. Why did God give me this experience, and how can I turn this into a story of resilience with calm, humility and forgiveness. What wisdom can I gain from this? I must be a fraud. I am not seeing these experiences with my dad as gifts from God. No way and no how. But, I continued to be pulled into deep reflection and praying to have God reveal it for me, and He did!

I can now see what gifts I would have desperately missed were it not for my dad. Had I not been desperate to leave my life behind for a respite, I never would have had the guts to venture to London without a place to live and to get a job on my own during college. Had I chosen to follow my heart and move to New York with my then fiancé, instead choosing a broken heart and ended engagement to stay behind because of my obligations to my dad, my husband and family would not be today. Had I learned the painting I owned was of great value earlier in my life (funny how it is God's time and not yours), I may have chosen a different path and left my dad behind. Had my parents had a better marriage, I would have missed the great moments living with my grandmother, Gigi, that imparted the spirit of creativity and adventure in me. Had I not been so desperate to grow my career to ensure a life of security for me and my dad, I would not have succeeded early in my career which is so foundational to my career and life today. Had I not inherited his smarts and sense of humor, who would I be today? And, more!

me and my dad, 1968

And, so I share this story with you. One that has been held in the shadows of my heart filled with anger, fear and self-pity is now revealing gifts of wisdom, thankfulness and blessings. I now recognize the guilt I have held tightly must be washed away by a shared responsibility between my dad and me. Thank you, God, for the blessings of this book, for revealing this wisdom, giving light to the lessons learned and understandings through the writing of this chapter. I am relieved, and I am glad to express that it is considerably better and healthier to accept each and every experience, no matter how painful, as gifts from God. It is the experiences collected in our lives with the resiliency with which we respond to them, and the appreciation for each we are given. It took turning 50 and this book for me to sincerely recognize this. Thank you, God, for my dad, who in spite of it all, I am deeply grateful and miss greatly.

Adrianne grew-up in Southern California with her parents. She graduated from Scripps College in Claremont, California. A few years after graduating from college, she moved to Dallas, Texas. She received a master's degree from Southern Methodist University and pursued coursework towards a PhD at Dallas Baptist University. Her career as a human resources and business leader expands nearly 30 years, and she is currently the Chief Human Resources Officer with Caliber Home Loans. The Dallas Human Resources association recognized her as HR Executive of the Year in 2013. She has authored many articles related to and has presented at many conferences on organizational culture and talent as a competitive differentiator.

Adrianne lives with her husband, son (15) and daughter (12) in Plano, TX. They are active as a family in their schools, community and church.

6

Swiping Right to Myself – Rediscovery of Self-Love

Malaina Davis

A couple of years after my heart had been crushed in what I'd call "my first adult (post-college)" relationship, I had finally healed and enjoyed enough of the single life to give myself another shot at making a connection with someone else. While that first post-college relationship can be summed up as an introduction to metropolitan nightlife, brunches, insecurity, cheating, and the existence of the 'financially dependent man', this time around was different. Whereas in that situation, I'm pretty sure the guy I was dating had aspirations of being my cheating house-husband, when I later met "James" it was a complete 180-degree turn for me. He seemed to have his financial bearings, we got along, he was fun, and though I had a ton of doubts about him because of differences in our lifestyles, I stayed around and eventually grew to love him.

To help put things in perspective, I love HARD. James and I had our issues, the main issue being that we were never actually in a real relationship with a title. We argued about the relationship issue all the time and he would combat me with the justification that we were happy and it was only me, being hung up on a title as a result of societal pressure which was messing up our unity and peace. He asked me time and time again how a title would change anything for us and even though I tried to explain it was more about our commitment to one another than the title, he never saw things from my perspective. I waited for him to come around, for years actually, arguing my points about commitment whenever I saw the opportunity. I left him a few times for a few months here and there hoping to spark motivation, but it didn't stick. He would contact me promising to change and even though about 90% of me didn't believe he could, just that measly 10% of hope kept me around.

I should've seen beyond what I wanted to and accepted the reality facing me. He hadn't changed at all since I'd initially met him, but I was all too willing to ignore the signs all around me. He was surprisingly consistent - just as selfish, unmotivated, and scandalous as he'd been since Day 1. I allowed myself to be manipulated, I shut out the opinions of others (even those closest to me), and I put my "situationship" on the pedestal it never deserved. I let my love for him blind me to what should have been obvious signs that he would never truly be committed: we didn't spend our actual holidays together (though we exchanged gifts), he made minimal effort to introduce me to his friends (including his countless female "besties"), he was super secretive, and indirectly avoided all opportunities to meet and engage with my family, among other tell-tell indicators. Though I wanted him to transform into my knight in shining armor, what I didn't realize then was that it was never intended to be his role. I wish I could say that I started giving recognition to these signs at some point earlier than I actually did. It wasn't until the 2nd time I'd taken him back, after about 3 months of not speaking to him at all, 2-years and some change into our relationship, and after a situation literally ran up and slapped me in the face that I finally turned up the volume on my woman's intuition which had been screaming out to me for years.

It was like tunnel-vision all over again. I heard the words clearly, "…my homegirl's been telling me about the guy she's been dating for a couple of months and I had no idea who he was until I saw his picture…girl, it's him. It's James and they're going on a date TONIGHT!" I felt my heart stop beating and my hands starting to shake. This couldn't be happening…AGAIN, keeping in mind that my last relationship had resulted in what I'd now characterize as a cheating ex. I told myself that this had to have been a mix-up because he would never do this to me considering he knew my past, all the intricacies of my emotions, and had been my best friend for the 2+ years I'd known him. He, of all people, knew my sensitivity to male disloyalty and lying. Be that as it may, it didn't change the fact that two days before my birthday, one of my longtime girlfriends had just called to break the horrific news that the guy I'd been "unofficially", but officially, dating for a couple years had not only been dating a friend of hers, but had also begun a sexual relationship with that friend, which as a by-product included taking her to places we'd often frequented, including our favorite "date night" restaurants and expensive outings.

There was a sinking pit in my stomach, but I had to know as much as my friend knew. He'd spent the entire weekend before with me, celebrating my birthday with my closest friends and family, which in itself was a rarity that I'd taken in the moment as a sign we were FINALLY moving forward. I tried to collect myself (with the occasional outburst), staying calm enough to ask my friend all she knew: where they were scheduled to go on their date, how long they'd been dating, if he'd been around her child, and everything that immediately came to mind. Essentially, I was prepping my case and readying myself for war. I found out he'd met her in a similar way to how he'd met me, through Tinder with a fateful swipe to the right.

Immediately following our conversation, I rushed to confront him and was met with lies. He lied until I cornered him with the facts that I had. He made me doubt for just a second that none of this was truly happening. He cried, but only to draw my sympathy and forgiveness. I blinked twice, snapped back to reality and pushed on with the facts I had, which were few but enough to motivate me to keep pushing forward. While usually a bit passive and polite, I forced myself to be assertive despite my internal hesitations. It was only then because I came forth backed by seemingly hard proof that his lies unraveled before me and he admitted to more than I'd even expected. I realized he was definitely a creature of habit and had a pattern of using dating sites and social media to make love connections. He had not only been dating a friend of a friend, but admitted he had been using dating apps (including the app I'd originally met him through) to connect with and date women around the city – starting intimate relationships with them until he felt that they were too invested with "feelings" and then tossing them aside. His explanation that I meant more to him than they did meant nothing to me. He tried to paint these women as "less than" because of how he'd decided to mislead and use them. He needed instant gratification that he was "the man", so he flaunted, wined, and dined women and used me for some level of actual love and support.

I initially blamed myself for having faith in him and believing all of the lies he'd told. It took just about a week before I looked at my situation and started to piece together where I'd went wrong, but more importantly how I was going to learn from the situation going forward. I felt like finally going through such a horrible, yet inevitable, experience with him freed me from our toxic situation. I'd been struggling with commitment from this man for years and because I loved him, I'd given up the battle for what I wanted and stayed in an imbalanced relationship. My desire to be married with children combined with an ultimate lack of confidence in myself drove me to continue my involvement with an unworthy man. We did not share the same family values and regardless of how I explained it, he didn't understand the value of a strong family unit. If I had recognized the significance of just that key difference alone, I could've saved myself some grief. Instead, I stayed in a situation where I constantly stressed about him at night, what he may be doing, who called or texted his cell phone, and whether I was doing enough to prove my worth. My intuition all along was telling me that he was unworthy, but I chose not to listen because I had created an idea that my kindness and willingness to love him would lead him to change for me. Little did I realize that his own impulses were more important to him than any impacts his actions could have on me.

This was my second notable experience where I'd let an unworthy man steal years of my life away. I later processed the similarities between he and the ex-boyfriend before him. He'd carefully disguised himself as a "good man", much like the first, but eventually (when cornered) came clean about who he truly was - a narcissist and a professional at hurting people with no remorse. He'd lived a double-life the entire time I knew him and rationalized that he'd only lied to me to protect my feelings, just another lesson I was able to walk away with: no love from a man will be ridden with lies under the justification of protection.

My upbringing helped me to develop an upmost respect and appreciation for the "traditional" family model – monogamy, marriage, and children – in that order. As an unmarried almost 30-something, it's now important for me to understand that the self-inflicted pressure to find a mate and begin to build one's own family is futile. As a God-fearing woman, I rediscovered peace in knowing that if being matriarch to my own family is part of my journey, I won't need to force it. I've had to come to grips with some level of recognition that it may be outside the scope of my purpose. With that understanding, I recognize an even greater importance of being happy with myself and my life. None of this is to say I've given up hope, however, my approach is different. Looking back, I can attribute some of my willingness to stay in my broken relationship with James, and even the relationship before him, to giving in to the pressures of time for fear of wasting it. In doing so, I compromised my own happiness.

I prayed A LOT after this situation and asked myself if I had become one of those people that only prayed when I need help. I even sat in church and felt like the pastor was preaching directly to me. While I don't remember the sermon word for word, I do remember the message: when negative things happen in life it's [my] duty to shine through and concentrate on the blessings [I've] been afforded by the grace of God. This situation happened and there is no changing it, however, I have control over how I allow this person, this situation, and these circumstances impact my life.

With maturity, I've learned the importance of forgiving but not forgetting. I do not hold on to the anger that comes along with a situation like this because I believe it would hinder my focus. I also don't believe it's my responsibility to hold on to the "what ifs" or "I should haves". My responsibility is to make sure that I'm growing and cutting things (or people) out of my life which hold me back from my purpose. To truly take away what I needed to in order to grow from this, I had to look within myself and recognize my own worth and strength. I began asking myself hard questions about the people that I want to be associated with. I found an ultimate value in my bond with my family. I refocused energy into my career. I took the sadness that came with this particular situation and used it as fuel towards my interests.

I refuse to give credit to those that hurt me for making me who I am today. I won't credit them for my successes. I won't honor or applaud them for being a vessel driving me closer to my potential. I definitely won't bow down to them in gratitude for making me stronger through their betrayals. However, I will acknowledge that the situations they put me through *changed* me. Those situations helped me to *remember* who I am – a queen. While difficult in the moment, this hard experience and others like it help me remember that if I walk with unwavering faith and the support of God, coupled with the support and love of my family, I'm unstoppable. Through allowing myself to fail in a way similar to how I have in the past, under slightly different circumstances, I was able to learn from my mistakes and draw strength, understanding, and trust towards myself. With all lessons learned I was able to walk away with no longer categorizing what I've been through as a failure, but instead reclassified as a blessing…

Born and bred in Arlington, TX but a true Cajun baby at heart (with strong ties to the great state of Louisiana), Malaina is a millennial middle-child and sibling to two gorgeous, charismatic, and intelligent sisters. Growing up in a two-parent household where joint prayers recited aloud before bed and family bike rides through the neighborhood were the norm, Malaina grew up with an unwavering, invaluable family bond, from which she draws strength and support.

She and her siblings played tennis throughout their upbringing and eventually Malaina was led to play through high school and later college on a full athletic scholarship to Grambling State University in Grambling, LA. It was there, at Grambling, Malaina was taught many important lessons, many of which promoted self-confidence as an intelligent minority with the power to be a difference-maker. It was also there where she cultivated a growing love for good friends, good music, seafood and frozen beverages.

After receiving a B.A. in Political Science from G.S.U. and while at home earning a Master in Public Administration at the University of Texas at Arlington, Malaina began to work towards developing her career and took a vested interest in Human Resources. Through a passion for all things HR and amazing mentorship from leaders over the course of her career thus far, she boasts a strong professional profile in the Corporate arena which she looks forward to expanding even further!

7
Empty

Calia Kimball

If I close my eyes, I can vividly remember sitting in a small beige classroom surrounded by a group of my peers. I am transported back to the church where I attended nearly every day of the week throughout my childhood. The lesson on this day was on the divine duty of motherhood. A lesson I had heard a hundred times before and would hear a hundred times again until I left the church. I grew up in a large Mormon family, surrounded by many other large families. I was never lacking in examples of how families were supposed to look in God's eyes. Growing up in this "family" centric ideology, I never doubted that I would be a mother. It was my divine purpose, and I didn't see many other paths than the one placed on the pedestal before me.

At around the age of 14, I became a woman and started my period. I can recall bleeding so heavily that the pads would become soaked within minutes. My periods came only a few times a year, and they often left me bedridden. At one point, my mother had me tag along to a sibling's doctor appointment to ask about my menstruation cycles. More as an afterthought, she mentioned it to the doctor on our way out. He glanced down at me and offered me birth control (which we never filled) to help minimize the bleeding. But it was his comment that has haunted me for years.

"You should get in with an ob-gyn to make sure there is nothing more serious going on."

His words planted a seed of self-doubt, crippling any confidence I had in my uterus and in my "divine duty" to bear children.

Like a lot of Mormon girls, I spent my teenage years babysitting children to make extra money. I enjoyed it so much that I ventured into daycare which, in turn, led me to become a full-time nanny.

I met my husband in 2002 at the end of my senior year of high school. It would not be until I was 22 that our relationship became more serious. In April of 2007, he proposed. To say I was elated, would be an understatement. We were blissfully unaware of what was to come.

That summer we suffered our first loss. At the time, I was working as a live-in nanny for a family I had come to love and cherish. I had suspicions that I might be pregnant. I took a few pregnancy tests that showed faint pink lines. I went to bed with some minor cramping that had come and gone throughout the day. The next morning, I woke up in agonizing pain. I became lightheaded at any sudden movement. As I sat up, I felt a warm gush of liquid between my legs. I threw back the blankets and saw a puddle of blood soaking the sheets. Cautiously I got out of bed. With every step I took, the blood ran down my legs. The room began to spin around me. I made it to the bathroom where I immediately started vomiting. My whole body seemed to be on fire. I laid down on the cold tile and passed out. I think I flashed out of consciousness for few minutes, though I could not be sure. I could hear the young boy I cared for in the hall. I called him to the bathroom door. I asked him to go downstairs to tell his step-dad that I was sick and unable to work. The cramping became more intense. I sat down on the toilet and felt a new gush of blood. I looked down in the water that was now bright red with blood. I realized instantly I had lost whatever life I had carried inside me for so brief a time.

Although it pains me to say, this would not be our only loss in the years to come. One after another after another, my body would not sustain the life we created together. My body refused to bring a child into the world, no matter how desperately we ached for it.

Our lives became routine. We married in the winter of 2007, my husband finished school, and we moved back to his small hometown. We spent those first few years as newlyweds getting to know each other and building our life together. We did not have a lot in terms of wealth, but we had our love and wanted children to share it with. Our time together quickly faded into years, and we still had no baby to show for it.

I took another nanny job for a beautiful little boy that I grew to adore. During my tenure with this family, I endured yet another devastating miscarriage. I came into work after a few days of recovery. I shuffled through our morning routine like clockwork. Like habit, I sat him on the floor to read some books before his morning nap. I looked down into his sweet face, as I had a hundred times before. His features were so similar to mine, wispy blonde hair and pale eyes. In public, we were often mistaken as mother and son. He gazed up at me with pure innocence in his eyes, and at that moment the thought came to my mind, "Would the child I lost look like this?" In that brief spell of longing, all my loss and grief came bubbling to the surface. The tears rolled down my cheeks and onto the top of his head. I knew the time had come. My heart could no longer bear to care for others' children while my arms remained empty. The realization of facing each day with a stark reminder of what I could not have was rending my mind and my soul into pieces.

Not long after that incident, in 2009, we made our first appointment with a professional. Our first stop was a family physician, where I voiced my concerns about my fertility (or lack of). The concerns were brushed off, and we were told to wait another year for results. At that point, we had been trying for three years.

Two more years flashed by without incident. I took a new job as an administrative assistant. While the job was not particularly satisfying, the daily monotony kept my mind busy from thinking of the children I still did not have. It was in the summer of 2011 that we made our second appointment to see if we could get any answers.

The appointment was at the only reproductive endocrinologist our small town offered. My stomach was in knots leading up to the consultation. I feared being told that I had no chance of having a biological child. We were led into a small office for our consultation. He was older, stern and unapproachable. He looked over the blood work and semen analysis. Everything looked fine, according to him. He proceeded to diagnose me with PCOS, a condition I had no signs or symptoms of. He then asked if he could do a transvaginal ultrasound. I froze. I looked to my husband for a brief moment for reassurance, then agreed.

My heart started to race. The doctor led me across the hall into a small room with an exam table and ultrasound machine. He told me to undress from the waist down and cover myself with a flimsy paper drape. He told my husband to wait outside. Realizing I was nervous, my husband opted to stay in the room. I removed my clothing before scooting up onto the exam table. My mouth was dry and my palms began to sweat. The room felt incredibly small. My past was rearing its head, and tiny tendrils of fear began snaking their way through my brain. As a victim of childhood sexual abuse, the thought of this strange man inserting a foreign object inside me was nauseating. There were two things that kept me from running and screaming from the building: my husband sitting protectively by my side and the thought that this could bring me one step closer to a baby.

There was a knock on the door, and the doctor came back into the room. He sat on a stool by my feet and immediately placed a hand on my thigh. My body bucked, and my pulse skyrocketed. I could hear him putting the lube on the wand,

and without warning he pushed the wand inside me. I cannot remember what he said in those next moments. I could not focus on his voice. I just wanted him to remove his hands and let me go. He pulled the wand out, and my body released the breath I did not realize I was holding. He put the wand back on the machine and stood. He told me to get dressed and come back into his office. As soon as he left the room, I pulled on my pants with shaky hands. I regained a small part of my dignity before walking back into his office. He lay out our options of IUI, a process where sperm is injected directly into the uterus. He did not have the capability of IVF (In Vitro Fertilization) in his clinic, so we would have to find another doctor if we chose that route. I was devastated by the severe lack of options. I wanted out of that office, so I mumbled my thanks and bolted for the door. I ran down the stairs to the street. The thought of him putting his hands on my body again made me physically ill. My husband and I both agreed that there was no way we would be stepping into that office again.

With the appointment with the RE leaving me shaky and unsettled, we decided to try a regular ob-gyn. Thinking back now, I realize how backward it all sounds. To say the appointment was ineffective would be putting it lightly. The doctor seemed inexperienced and, frankly, rude. She told us that if we could not afford to get treatment, we probably should not have children at all. A comment I would hear time and time again on our journey to parenthood. After explaining our situation, she diagnosed me with DOR (Diminished Ovarian Reserve). She prescribed us Clomid, a relatively common fertility medication to induce ovulation. We would proceed over the next six months to do four cycles of Clomid without ultrasounds to monitor follicle count. I would later learn that unmonitored medicated cycles were unsafe. Not only would I take this medication without any monitoring, reaching the clinic for any help at all was arduous. On Clomid, my cycles became 70 days or longer. My body was physically and mentally exhausted from the side effects. After our last cycle had failed, we did not return to the clinic.

Days turned into months, and months turned into years. In late 2012, I changed careers and moved into 911 dispatch. A job I felt was as rewarding as it was distracting of my still empty womb. My soul felt fragile from repeated loss, and I did not know if we would ever reach the point of trying again. Seven months into my new job, my whole world came crashing down around me.

I was working a graveyard shift and had just been promoted. I left work smiling yet tired. I arrived home the next morning and began changing into my pajamas. My phone rang. I did not usually receive calls from anyone but my sister. Surprised, I looked down onto the screen. The number displayed was my father's. It was not common for him to call me on the phone. I was tired and contemplated sending him to my voicemail. But a slight feeling of unease made changed my mind. The next words I heard brought my world to a screeching halt. My sister, my best friend, my confidante, my other half was gone. She had died while I was working. I hung up the phone, and my knees hit the floor. I was so stunned that I had not even begun to cry. I was frozen. My husband was asleep in our bedroom, and my body seemed to move on it's own accord. I crawled across the bed, and he woke. He looked questioningly at my face, and as I looked back, I began to sob. Heart-wrenching sobs from deep within came tearing out. Once I began, I could not stop. My heart already bore deep cracks from the loss of my unborn children. Coupled with my inability to conceive it had ruptured into a tiny million splintered pieces. The grief tore through my body; my chest felt empty and sore. My husband held me tightly in his arms.

The next few days passed in a blur. I remember asking for vodka and orange juice - anything to make me forget the nightmare I was living. I remember coming to, sobbing on the bathroom floor. Alcohol could not heal this wound. The world was no longer stable. I felt off balance. My sister was my best friend. We never went a day without talking. She knew all my darkest secrets and knew intimately of my struggle with conceiving. Next to my husband, she was my world. With her gone, I was adrift. I had no anchor, I was sinking into the dark and did not know if I would ever break the surface again.

The next year saw no progress on the baby front. I was still drowning. I was swimming upstream against a tide of grief that I could not surmount. At one of my lowest moments, I told my husband I could not continue to try for something we might never attain. All the sorrow had built up inside, but

I had to do something. I had to find myself again. I had to find some semblance of myself inside this dark storm that I had become.

Then one long night at work I was reading a blog on solo traveling. Two quotes jumped out at me. The first said, "Sometimes the journey has to be traveled alone in order to appreciate the strengths that lie deep inside you." The second read, "Travel not to find yourself but to remember who you've been all along." The words resonated with me. I had to find my strength. I had to remember what I wanted and why. I decided that getting away might do me good. One of the last conversations I had with my sister had been us discussing winning a trip to the Adriatic. She had a list of all these places she wanted to go. I decided I needed to go for my self, but I also wanted to go to honor her.

That summer I packed my bags. I printed out a few copies of a picture I had taken of my sister and I left. I landed in Paris with only a few words of French and not knowing a soul. I spent the next two weeks traveling alone with just my thoughts, my journal, and a picture of my sister. I cried, I begged, I laughed, and I grieved. Traveling made me find joy in things I thought I would never have joy in again. I faced my fears and gained confidence. I returned home, and I told my husband I was not ready to be finished. I wanted a child and would do whatever it took.

At the end of the year, we found a new reproductive endocrinologist in Denver, a six-hour drive from our small town. The process was long. We had to wait months for all the testing hoops they made us jump through. We were relieved to find out that both previous diagnoses were incorrect. We were now officially, unexplained. The doctor suggested intrauterine insemination, and we fervently agreed. We had our first IUI in August of 2015.

I was put back on Clomid to stimulate my follicles with a trigger shot to release the egg. We drove the six hours to Denver. I was apprehensive and trying not to cling to hope. Hope had let me down so many times. The next morning we drove to the clinic. I was holding my husband's sperm in a small container in my lap, praying we would not get pulled over. The nurse met us at the front and led us back to the exam room. She had me undress and get onto the table. An unfamiliar female doctor came in and explained the process. She showed me the sample and had me verbally confirm that it was my husbands. I lay back on the crinkled white sheet. She prepared the instruments while I shut my eyes. I had to mentally steel myself for the oncoming invasion of my body. It was just a moment before she announced she was done. Now we would wait. In two weeks I could test again - the same day as my sister's birthday. Surely this was a sign that it was going to work. "It could not be more perfect", I thought to myself. I sat on the toilet holding the test in my trembling hands. I could not bring myself to look down. What if it was negative? What if all the work to get to this point had been for nothing? I looked down. One pink line amidst a stark white background. My uterus had failed again. I was not pregnant.

My husband and I decided to try again right away. We started the process over. I took the pills. I did the ultrasounds that made me sick and brought old wounds to the surface over and over again. The pills did not work. My follicles did not react. We tried a stronger dose. Nothing. My body refused to cooperate. Our doctor told us that I was a weak responder. She explained to us that our best bet was IVF (In Vitro Fertilization), a process that would cost us thousands of dollars. We were back to the drawing board. We began our research again. The clinic we loved did not have a guarantee program, and the prices were higher than we had expected. I went to my support group for help. A clinic on the east coast stood out from the rest. They had a great program that would give us multiple IVF cycles. If we did not take home a live baby, we would get our money back. I flew to the east coast in October of 2016 for some more procedures. My husband flew out shortly after and we were given the green light to move forward with IVF.

Now, we are in a holding pattern. My husband with his teaching job and I in my government job, we are not exactly wealthy. We can afford to raise a child, but coming up with the amount for IVF up front is going to take some time. Infertility treatment is not covered by insurance. It is not a guarantee and by no means a walk in the park. With every appointment, I have to confront the trauma from my past. I feel broken all over again, vulnerable, and feel like I have no control over my body. I'm looking at even more needles, more invasive procedures, and potentially more heartbreak. But I'm not ready to give up. This story is not over.

Life has not turned out at all like I imagined. This journey has not been easy. I have gained friends and I have lost them. Friends who cannot fathom why being around children is unbearable. Who can not understand when they tell me they are pregnant, I am happy for them but heartbroken for me. I have taken on habits to protect myself. I avoid Facebook announcements like the plague. I've learned to map out stores before I go in so I can avoid the baby aisles. I respectfully decline baby showers, and I become a hermit on Mother's Day.

I can clearly recall Mother's Day as a young adult. The church leaders would have every woman stand and present them with flowers. This practice categorizes all women as mothers, instead of identifying that women can play many important roles. I think of the women who are struggling like me sitting in those congregations today. I think of the flowers they receive and feel their sorrow.

Next to the anniversary of my sister's death, Mother's Day is the hardest day of the year. I have been lapped multiple times over by friends I grew up with. Those who have now had 5 or 6 children in the 11 years I have been trying. I watch my husband hold a baby or play with kids, and I feel heart-wrenching despair. I deeply envy the women, who conceive without even trying. With such despair comes self-preservation, and despite my instinct to love completely, I build walls to protect myself. I disconnect from the situations that cause me pain, and with those situations, the people I once cared about.

However, my journey has not been without some good. I have made my fair share of mistakes. Those mistakes have made me learn and grow. As a child, I was taught that motherhood was the most important thing you could do. That motherhood was the central tenet of womanhood. This belief made me doubt my value as a woman. Motherhood is so highly regarded and socially rewarded. It stands as a sort of surrogate for femininity. I have had to relearn the meaning of womanhood and my place in it. I have felt broken, less than whole. I have been isolated, alone and misunderstood. I have learned that my grief, my sadness, my pain have molded me into a stronger version of me. I have learned to see myself as someone with determination and bravery instead of someone who is inadequate. My infertility has ignited new passions and self-purpose.

I may have an empty womb, and empty arms, but I can still be fulfilled. I have helped raise children, I have created life if even for a fleeting moment. I have grieved for children I have never met, and for a future I might never have. I have loved, and I have lost. These experiences have made me fundamentally accept who I am in the world. If at the end of this journey my womb remains empty, I will still be standing. I am no less of a woman, wife, sister or aunt. My value and worth is so much more than my ability to bear children. I am a survivor. I am complete.

Calia Kimball is a freelance writer and infertility blogger. She published her first short story during her freshman year of high school. Calia has been an emergency 911 dispatcher for the past 5 years. She is an avid traveler, who enjoys cooking and exploring the outdoors during her time off. She lives with her husband and two huskies in rural Southwest Colorado.

8

You're Enough®

Dawn Thompson

Y ou're worthless, you're so lazy, and you're never going to amount to anything." That is what I was told and how I felt most of my life. I felt unworthy, unloved and that I was just not enough.

At the age of five, I can remember when my mom stood me on the back bumper of her car and said, "See those apartments over there? That's where our new home is going to be. You and I are going to live there, and your daddy won't be coming with us. He is moving out of town."

I thought, "What!?" We were leaving our home. The place where I belonged with my mom and my dad and my friends in the neighborhood. But most of all I remember thinking, "Will I ever see my daddy again?" I remember thinking to myself, "Is this my fault? Could I have been a better little girl?"

We moved into a one-bedroom apartment situated in a complex that was known for housing the singles' partying community. My world as I knew it was falling apart. I didn't understand it all. It happened so fast, leaving me confused and heartbroken.

My mom began seeing someone who was a partying man. Eventually he moved in with us, which put me on the couch. Not only did I feel like I lost my dad, but felt like I was losing my mom too. Her boyfriend drank a lot and was verbally abusive. It made life hectic for my mother and me. I was miserable and scared. One day my mom and her boyfriend took me to my grandparents' for a sleepover because she said they were going out of town. I remember when they came back home my mom was so excited and said they had got married. The man who was so mean to me was now my step-dad. I remember as we pulled out of the driveway of my grandparents' house, my thoughts were "He is so mean and now he is going to forever live with us and there is nothing I can do about it."

I became a very confused, sad, and lonely child. I remember being in our small kitchen staring at the dark colored wood cabinets and overhead florescent lights thinking of how I was going to get rid of this emptiness I felt. I remember thinking, "I want to eat!" This is when my unhealthy relationship with food began. I thought it was my friend. I turned to food looking for comfort and love, trying to connect. Now looking back, I realize I gave food so much power. I would get in trouble for eating too much at meals or snack time, so I began to sneak food and hide it. With the weight packing on, I began to feel even more sad and unworthy. My step-dad would tell me:

"You're overweight and worthless."

"You're never going to amount to anything." "You're lazy."

I also began to tell myself these things. Once I started repeating them, I believed them. Once I started to believe them, I became them.

Like my mom, my real father also remarried and moved back to town. Crazy enough, we all ended up living in the same neighborhood. I was only five blocks from my dad and his new wife and her three children. My mom and step-mom did not get along, and my parents would argue about that. They would argue each month about the $50.00 my dad owed in child support. I remember my mom saying to my dad, "Is she not worth $50.00 a month to you?" So, I began to wonder, "Am I not even worth $50.00 to him?" This crushed my already low self-esteem and the way that I viewed myself.

Since we lived in the same neighborhood as my dad, it didn't take long for me to realize that he had to drive past our house every day around the same time. For days, I made sure I was outside playing in the front yard at that time. As soon as I saw his car turn onto our street, I would run to the curb, waving my hands for him to stop. Each day, he would look straight ahead and continue driving. I began to think to myself, "He must not love me."

School continued to be a place of struggle and heartache. I was labeled "fat" by my classmates, which made learning difficult. I was placed in remedial classes. Kids became even meaner. I was known as the fat remedial Dawn.

A few years later, a tornado destroyed our home and we had to move again. We bought a house in the same town, and I started at a new school and made new friends. They taught me how to not let people bully me. As I transitioned into high school, most of these friends and I went our separate ways. I began to hang out with tougher crowds who like me were carrying pain too advanced for their age. By surrounding myself with these people I thought I became tougher. I became interested in boys, partying, and cared way too much about what other people thought of me. My friends were using drugs, so I thought if I did them too I would fit in. I started using sex to gain attention from boys. When having sex I felt loved, pretty, and for that short time, I felt I mattered to someone. I then developed the attitude, "You may not love me, but you will love to have sex with me." What I did not realize was that with each partner I left behind a piece of my soul making me feel even more broken. I was crying out for attention and for someone to love me, love me, love me... *please*.

When I was 17, my mom and step-dad separated. I loved having my mom to myself again and our lives didn't seem so chaotic which I was really enjoyed. Until the day she took him back. At that point, I had decided that I was moving out. I got my own apartment, I quit school just months before graduating, and I ended up working three different jobs to make ends meet.

I had little time for a social life, but I met a man that I worked with and developed a relationship with him. He was tall and handsome. He was an amazing man. He treated me with respect and was the most normal person I had ever dated. One night after a long and chaotic day at work, he surprised me with my favorite meal – spaghetti – for dinner and he dressed in a nice suit. He planned a whole night of pampering me and no one had ever treated me like that. He was always very thoughtful and sweet. I remember thinking to myself that I would never find anyone else like him and I must marry him. When I was 22, we married. He was everything a woman could have wanted in a husband. He was very intelligent and caring. My family and friends adored him. He encouraged me to follow my dreams of going to school and opening my own business, which was a nail salon. Although this was a perfect environment for a marriage to thrive, I didn't know what to do with "normal" and someone treating me with respect. I created problems where there were none, sabotaging the relationship between us. After only two years of marriage, we got a divorce.

Over the next 8 years or so, I continued working long and hard, growing my nail salon business and career. I decided to further my career, and went to school for massage therapy. After graduating from massage school, I purchased a cute little cottage that I turned into a day spa and salon. During this time, I also became an educator for an aromatherapy company that allowed me to travel.

During my travels I fell in love with the beaches and scenery of Florida. I was planning to open another spa located there. I had already found a place to live and was ready to go. I went to a fundraiser to tell some friends good-bye, and there I ended up meeting a handsome blue-eyed cowboy.

Needless to say he caught my attention and I found myself wanting to stay in town. So I decided to let go of the dream of going to Florida. After all, I was still searching for someone to love me and I had found him. We had been dating for a few months when I found out I was pregnant. So, off to Vegas we went to get married. We felt it was the right thing to do since we were expecting a child together. He was kind with a loving heart, but we both made poor decisions out of our brokenness. We were each doing things to mask our pain; I ate my problems away and he drank his away. I was starting to repeat the chaotic lifestyle in which I grew up.

One of the great things that we did in our marriage was bring our kids into this world. After our first child I gained a lot of weight and tipped the scales at almost 300 pounds. I was beyond miserable; unhealthy, tired, and unhappy. I was working non-stop and was mentally and physically exhausted. I was hoping for something to change and stop carrying the weight around. I had battled this weight struggle for my whole life. I wanted so desperately to be thin, trying one diet after another failing time after time.

God has always been a big part of my life, but I really started praying hard at that time. I finally felt led to have gastric bypass surgery. While this surgery was a solution to the physical aspect of weight loss, it didn't change the psychological battles taking place in my head. I always told myself that if I were skinny, everything would be perfect. I thought that if I were skinny I would finally be happy and the problems in my marriage would subside. With the weight dropping off, my husband and I grew further apart. I wanted affection and communication. I wanted him to spend more time with me and tell me what I meant to him. I wasn't getting the attention from him that I thought weight loss would give me. But I did start to get attention from others, and I began to accept love from outside of my marriage. I was left confused, hurt, unhappy, and full of shame. I never thought I would be the sort of person to commit adultery, but I felt empty and desperate to fill the void in my soul.

During this time one of my friends came to me with an opportunity for help. I was excited for the chance to get better and took her up on the offer. What I didn't realize was that she was sending me to a rehab facility called Shades of Hope in Buffalo Gap, Texas. Though I felt broken, I thought there was no way I needed rehab. In fact, I felt like I above it. In spite of my misgivings, it became a turning point in my life. I learned skills to help combat not only my troublesome relationship with food, but also my need to feel loved by anyone and everyone.

One exercise in particular still stands out to me. I learned I was a 'crumb chaser.' Simply put, I dated men who would throw me just enough crumbs to keep me around and I thought this was acceptable. I didn't understand at the time that I was deserving of more than just someone else's crumbs. This exercise was life-changing for me because I also learned that my children had a higher chance of picking up my same habits and were at risk of constantly searching for love in all the wrong places. I knew that I never wanted my children to repeat my mistakes.

We continued to work on our marriage for about a year, but came to recognize that we were better apart. Our marriage ended in divorce. We did our best to assure to our children that it was not their fault. It was important to us for the kids' sake that not only we remain friends but also that our families still interact. Over time we seemed to emotionally grow closer than when we were married.

As time passed, I was longing for adult interaction and tired of being at home so out into the dating world I ventured once again. I would find myself out on a date thinking, "Are you someone I would want around my children?" Every one was a resounding "No." I became sick and tired of being sick and tired. Getting dressed up and ready for another let-down date. I returned to what I had learned at Shades of Hope. I knew I had to face my fear of being alone and that everything I wanted was on the other side of fear.

From that moment on, I WAS DONE! It was time to make a change. I started to look more to God to help me and show me a sign. I prayed relentlessly and vowed to stop settling for less. I promised God I would wait for what He had planned for me. I asked of Him, "Please, help me get it right and show me what love really is." I learned life would give me what I ask of it, and I had not been asking for much. I stopped trying to manage my painful past by revisiting it. I decided I was not taking my childhood suffering into any more of my adulthood. I had longed my whole life for love, searching everywhere for it, whether it was with food, drugs, shopping, work or people. As I began healing my inner wounded child, I realized I was scared, hurt, and not allowing love in.

I set out into the self-discovery world and submerged myself in learning what it meant to have self-esteem, self-worth, and self-love. I learned to raise my standards and work on my identity issues. I discovered the biggest enemy was the one living in my head. I also realized all the struggles in my past were necessary to live out God's purpose for me. I have so much gratitude to God for my journey, the good and the bad. My God given purpose is to share my past so hopefully it doesn't become someone else's future.

I started to share my story with friends, then friends of friends, and before I knew it, I was being asked to be the keynote speaker at self-discovery sessions. I shared my passions, my trial, my journey, and how I overcame my inner childhood demons. I was finally able to articulate my journey which became my most powerful healing tool.

One of the first things I had to learn was the valuable lesson of forgiveness. Forgiveness returned my power. Most importantly, I had to forgive myself of my past. Forgive my parents and others who I felt hurt me. People who are hurting will hurt other people. I refused to carry the hurt. When I forgave the people and the circumstances that hurt me and harmed me, they no longer controlled me. I knew that if I continued to stay in the pain I would self-destruct again. Staying in my hurt and pain led me to eating too much, engaging in bad relationships, and hurting others. I learned that I needed to forgive others the way that I know God forgives me. I realized that my parents did the best that they could with the resources they had. I stopped blaming them for all the bad things in my life and gave my blame a different meaning. Instead, I gave them credit for all the good things, such as raising me to be here today. I had been incapable of love from all the pain and disappointments I had experienced in life; I was withholding love from others and myself. I now know I am capable and deserving of loving others and myself. I now allow that love in.

I had to ask myself what meaning was I giving other things in my life. Was there a problem area that I could give a different meaning? I always remind myself that life is happening *for* me and not *to* me. I God has put me in my situations to change my heart. I have learned to take my struggles to God before I take it to anyone else. Prayer is the most important conversation of the day and so is the conversation I have with myself. Some of the most important words that come out of my mouth come after "I am..."

In the past, some of the words that came after "I am," for me were horrible. When I looked in the mirror I said such things as, "You're fat." "Your thighs are too big." and "Your butt is too flat." I would constantly look and point out my flaws.

Now, in my mirror time I tell myself that I love my thighs; they have carried me through this life and allowed me to create some amazing experiences. I look deep into my soul and say, "Dawn, I am proud of you." "I believe in you." "I trust you." "I love you." and "There is no one person like me and I am enough." At first I didn't believe it, but I kept on until now I know it, believe it, and live it. I learned how to love my reflection, and really look inside myself. Truth is about bringing attention to yourself every day. Say to yourself, "I am beautiful as I am." What are you saying to yourself?

I not only do this awesome activity with myself but I also partake in mirror time with my children. I reinforce my love and God's love; that they are perfectly made in his image, and that is their power. Watching their reaction to this unconditional love is priceless.

I would love to encourage you if you are struggling with not feeling your worth or feeling unloved, to do some mirror time and show yourself the self-love that you deserve. Be kind to yourself. After all, you can't properly take care of something that you don't love. Another amazing tool I use is a self-love journal. I get everything out of my head and into the journal. Three pages a day keeps the doctor away. As I write, I am sending love and gratitude to God and myself. I write out all the things I love about me. I celebrate me and my awesome life and how I learned to **FLY**: Faithfully Love Yourself.

All that love I had been looking for all these years was in me the whole time. I gave myself permission to be me. I stopped wondering and caring what others thought of me. Most people don't even know what to think of themselves, so why look to them to validate me by looking or dressing a certain way, or driving a fancy car, or what is the popular clique to hang out with? I learned that trying to get approval from others would almost always leave me feeling that I was not enough. There is nothing wrong with wanting to look a certain way or have nice things, but it is important to do them for you and nobody else. Know it is okay to not be liked by everyone and it is okay to be different. Your vibe will attract your tribe. I look back at my life with all my failures and disappointments, and I see clearly now. I see them as bright experiences that have guided me to where I am today. I feel deep acceptance from myself. No need to run from it anymore. I stopped trying to manage my painful past. It was time to say goodbye to this part of my journey and to let it go. I now know my worth. I am still a single mom rocking life, living it to the fullest and working on some big exciting things!

When I got out of my own way and started listening to God, I began to believe in myself. If you believe in yourself, you have 100% of the people that you need on your side. We are all unique and on a journey. We all have a book of life to write. We get to decide how our story will read. Will you have a book that gathers dust on the shelf or will yours be a best seller?

My journey wasn't easy. The concept of changing is easy, it's the work that can be difficult. But it's harder still to stay in a place where we as a person cannot grow. We were created for greatness, abundance, and joy. If your inner you is calling, don't silence it. Get curious, celebrate, and embrace the amazing person that you are! I am proud of myself, that I have worked diligently to overcome many struggles in my life. I would love to say that I am done working on me. However, I am still learning and working on myself everyday, and in every way I am getting better and better. I will work on myself until the day I leave this earth. After all, I am the best project I will ever work on.

While on this amazing journey I started the worldwide You're Enough® movement. My mission is to inspire as many lives as possible to let them know they are worthy and loved. If while on my You're Enough® journey, I am able to help one person, then I will be fulfilled.

My Resiliency Lessons:

1. **Give it to God** – Giving all my hurt and pain to God was the only way I could even begin the process of healing my body and my soul. No matter what you're up against, remember that there is nothing greater than the God we serve. Every day as you wake up, put on your *Godfidence*.

2. **The importance of forgiveness** – In order to truly move on, you must learn to forgive yourself and forgive others. Holding on to those negative emotions will not help you

reach your destination of greatness. Ask the people who you feel you have harmed to forgive you. Also forgive the people you feel have harmed you, whether they have asked forgiveness or not. You no longer need justice from them. Allow yourself to forgive and let it go. You are only one decision away from a totally different life.

3. **Have a love affair with yourself** – Look in the mirror and learn to see yourself through God's eyes instead of your own or anyone else's. Have a love journal and reflect on all your amazing qualities. We are perfect because we are made in His image. I would love to encourage you, if you are struggling with not feeling your worth or feeling unloved, to do some mirror time and show yourself the self-love that you deserve. Be kind to yourself. After all, you can't properly take care of something that you don't love. Another amazing tool I use is a self-love journal. I get everything out of my head and into the journal. Three pages a day keeps the doctor away. As I write, I am sending love and gratitude to God and myself. I write out all the things I love about me. I celebrate the awesome life I have been blessed with. You are one of a kind... embrace it and learn to **FLY**: Faithfully Love Yourself®.

4. **Scratch your record** – Understand your patterns so that you can stop them and learn to look at things from a new perspective. Stop the negative thoughts playing over and over in your head, and turn them into a beautiful love song that you have written for yourself. If you have something in your life bringing you distress, don't judge it or yourself.

Give it attention, and ask God why this is showing up in your life. Don't resist it; ask what good can come from it.

5. **Choose Joy**- We all tend to search outward for things to find our joy. Who or what will make us feel good? Examples: Are you looking for comfort in eating, drinking alcohol or doing drugs? Fulfillment in shopping... Acceptance in being a people pleaser... Satisfaction in a relationship... All in trying to find happiness, peace & joy. The only One that can truly bring you happiness, peace, joy and satisfy the human heart is the One who created it.

6. **You're Enough**® - No matter what anyone else says, no matter what challenges you face, you were created to do whatever you want in this life! Love yourself enough to be yourself. If your inner you is calling, don't silence it. After all, how far can you run from yourself? There is something in you that the world needs. Get curious, celebrate, and embrace the amazing and beautiful person you are. One of the best projects you will ever work on is yourself. This life is 100% your responsibility. You're Enough.

Dawn Thompson an award-winning and passionate businesswoman, keynote speaker, self-discovery coach and a single mother. Dawn has been a success in the beauty industry for over twenty-four years, owning and operating Spa Bella Inc. She has two non-profit organizations, Adopt-A-Box and Operation Spa Kids. These organizations provide haircuts, clothing, personal hygiene products and mentoring for children and teens.

In her keynotes, Dawn shares her own struggles and adversities in both her business and personal life experiences. Dawn has transcended her circumstances to become a leader on transformational changes as well as an in-demand inspirational speaker. She is living proof that you can change your life in an instant. She wakes you up to the possibilities of life and understanding the reason God gave you breath. She motivates individuals to achieve their personal and professional goals. She is passionate about helping you find your joy, loving and connecting with yourself and others. She believes that you can be fulfilled with life and enjoy it by learning to have inner peace, and start living it to the fullest.

Dawn Thompson will inspire you with her life changing message that **You're Enough®** while teaching you to **FLY – Faithfully Love Yourself®**.

Contact Info:
Website: youreenough.club
Facebook: @youreenoughmovement
Instagram: @YoureEnoughMovement

9

You're Fired!
My Journey From
A Tailspin to
Aerial Spins

Rhonda Nichols

In October of 2013, I heard those dreaded words, "you're fired". Well, not exactly. The words I heard were more like, "We are reorganizing and your services are no longer needed." But, the essence is the same. YOU NO LONGER HAVE A JOB OR A STEADY PAYCHECK OR HEALTH BENEFITS OR A MEANS TO SUPPORT YOURSELF OR YOUR FAMILY!!

I had been with my company for 5 years and just received a really good year-end review with an above average bonus. I was connected with a good internal network and great relationships with the teams and leaders I supported. So, I was more than caught off guard and it began to take hold of my psyche from the moment the dreaded phone call began.

This was not the first time I had been caught in a "reorganization," nor are the logistics of 'firing' meetings foreign to me. I had been on the other side of this discussion countless times in my 25 years as a Human Resources professional. That was an unfortunate part of my job. I worked with business leaders to help them plan workforce changes, reductions, moves and terminations.

Now the tables were turned and the meeting was for me. I was in shock and almost immediately all the normal fears set in. How would I continue to pay my mortgage, my car payment, all the utility bills, and keep my family fed? I was a single mom and sole financial provider for 2 kids. The weight of these responsibilities were feeling heavier than ever. The only way that I had provided for my family had just been cut off. This one act, those few unexpected words, set me into an emotional tailspin for which I was not prepared .

As an only child, my teenage parents divorced before I was potty trained. I grew up knowing that marriages weren't guaranteed to last and dads didn't always stick around. During all of my school years, I watched my mom work all day and take college classes at night. This had a dramatic influence on me as she was a model of how giving up was not an option. Earning a living, taking care of your child and continuing to grow was all achievable. But, it also helped me to set up many belief systems for my protection. One of the core beliefs I held dear to myself was that regardless of my marital status, I needed to be able to provide for myself. Additionally if I got my college degree and found a good job at a stable company, I would be financially stable. But I found myself in a place where I had two degrees, was working for a stable company, yet I was not secure. My job and my regular paycheck no longer existed. As I went to sleep that night, I was in shock, worrying about what my next steps would be, and praying when I woke up this was all a really bad dream.

After I got the kids off to school the next morning, I sat down to take inventory of how bad things really were. I started with finances. I had been given a severance package equivalent to 6 months of pay and benefits. Since that was being paid out in a lump sum in November, after Uncle Sam took his share, at best, I would end up with about 3 months' pay to work with. Three months is not very long when you have no other income and no foreseeable way to bring money in. I looked at my debt load, savings, and retirement funds. All in all, it wasn't as bad as it could have been. I had some time and some money to help with my transition into a new paycheck.

A new paycheck! Where would that come from? I started to think about new job options. I began to read job postings for HR positions in my town and all across the country. I started thinking of companies in my local market that might need my skills, where I could possibly do contract work. That is when the enormity of my layoff truly hit me. This wasn't only a financial impact, but this was a major emotional jarring! That emotional jarring led to lots of self doubt and doubt in my abilities. I mean why would my previous employer fire me if I was able to perform the tasks they needed? My tailspin of self doubt got faster and faster…. Less than 24 hours before, I was confident in my ability. I was a high performer in a company who prided itself on hiring star talent. I had the power to decide my actions, my value and my worth. And now, it felt like that power had been stripped from me. Asking myself what companies might want my skills made me start to think of the skills I had to offer, which then turned to doubts of all of my abilities.

Before I allowed this tailspin to drain me of all my energy and put me into a depression that would be hard to climb out of, I had to get out fast. I closed my eyes and asked myself, "what if life wasn't happening to me, but instead happening for me?" Tony Robbins asked this question in one of his life changing events I had previously attended. It seemed to be just the question to start me thinking of better questions and coming up with better answers.

I spent the next few days studying; really analyzing what my strengths were, what I enjoyed doing, and what I didn't enjoy. I began collecting all my previous year-end reviews, appraisals, the atta-girl notes, my completed assessments (Myers Briggs, Strengthfinders, DISC, etc.) and any other written feedback to give me a balanced perspective. I looked at all of them and started to identify patterns. What was I good at? Where did I shine? How did others perceive me? Again, another good question to explore. I sat down at my Facebook and created a post: I am starting to think more about my personal brand and need your help. What is one word that describes me? The results I got were magnificent; giving, loving, capable, intelligent, witty, grace, fun, calm, quick-study, strategic, resourceful, strong, peacemaker, adaptable, innovative, creative, dedicated, ambitious, team builder, RESILIENT......

These words sounded much better to me than the words swirling in my head as part of the internal meaning I gave to "you're fired". My internal words sounded much more like; not enough, not worthy, poor performer, no good, unwanted, unskilled. I liked my Facebook list much better.

This was the first time in a long time that I took time and really focused on me. I got my kids out the door in the morning and designed the entire day as I wanted. No boss telling me what time to be at work and what my day's priorities were. I plotted my information on a chart that I affectionately called my Miles of Smiles Line. (see insert). I had seen similar charts in on-line training courses to help identify product benefits, and thought this modification could help me gauge what was important to me. So, I listed the things that I did daily or weekly, and where they fell based on my dislikes (below the smile line), my likes (above my smile line) and my loves (at my miles of smiles line).

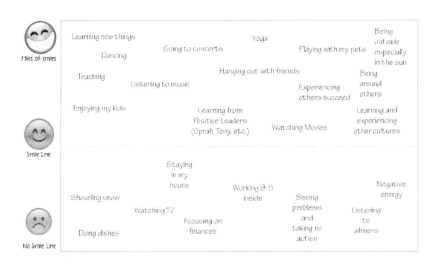

This was a very telling one page summary of my life. Most of my waking minutes were spent on activities below my smile line. I was spending my time going through the motions of life and I needed to start getting connected to my emotions… and my smiles. As I looked at my chart, one thing that struck me was the love I had for many things that I hadn't experienced in a very long time. I realized how much I enjoyed concerts and how long it had been since I had attended one. And as luck would have it, Pink was performing near me that weekend.

Pink has always been someone that I was intrigued by. I love her energy and her independence and strength. And, having seen some of her performances on TV, I knew how much of a BEAST she is. She performs aerial acts 30 feet in the air, bounds across the stage at a full sprint and dances like crazy. All this while she is maintaining breath control, singing, and occasionally playing instruments. She is a bucket of energy, joy and fun. I decided right then and there that I wanted some of that. I loved how free and happy she appeared. She had a genuine love for life and turned that into play time for herself and her band, in front of thousands of on looking fans who paid to see it.

I went home from the concert that night with my passion and excitement about this next chapter in my life bubbling over. I barely slept. Pink had renewed my hope for life after Corporate America and made me think outside the box; that there were more ways to earn a living than in a 9 to 5 corporate environment. One of the things that amazed me at the concert was Pink's ability to perform in aerial silks and net hammocks. It looked fun! And combined elements of dance, fitness and strength, I knew I needed to explore that more. The next morning I searched for Aerial Yoga classes and found a studio 60 miles away that offered a class. I signed up for that class. Little did I know that this would be a pivotal point in my journey.

I walked into a small yoga studio and was escorted to a room in the rear of the building with 4 hammocks hanging from the ceiling. A petite and welcoming dancer stood at the front of the room and two other people were already sitting in the hammocks. I soon found out they were cocooned in frog pose. The instructor helped me adjust the hammock to a height appropriate for me, and showed me how to maneuver into that pose. She reassured me that if I had any questions or any problems with any poses that she would be happy to help. From that first frog pose through the first inversion in the hammock, I was hooked. I loved it. I loved everything about it. I knew this was what I had to do. As I drove back home on my aerial yoga high, I daydreamed about a business that allowed me to teach others this skill; to empower others through life transitions both literally (through aerial yoga positions) and figuratively (as they took on the fear of the unknown).

I woke up early and spent the entire next day visualizing this business. What the studio would look like, who the clients would be, what they would expect and what they would receive. As excited and hopeful as I was, I also had doubts and fears that kept me in check. This was all really outside of my comfort zone: I didn't have a Yoga Teaching Certification, I was new to Aerial Yoga, I hadn't run a successful business of my own, and there were so many things that would have to be done to start a business from scratch. I didn't know where to start.

So, what do I do now? Do I put this vision on the back burner and come back to reality; start applying for corporate HR jobs. I also began to explore franchise ownership and do deep dives into their business models considering what might work in my geographical area. I read and listened to CDs from others who have figured out a system to get rich. I played the lottery. Yes, I did all of those things. But, the two most important things that I did during this window of fear and uncertainty was to continue to listen to my passion, and sign up to attend a 7 day seminar led by Life Coach Tony Robbins.

Since my subconscious mind did not allow me to give up on my passion, I would find myself scanning empty retail space looking for a perfect studio whenever I was out and about around town. I also found all the local yoga studios and started to take classes. Even though it wasn't aerial yoga, it did give me a feel for the local market. Through the Internet, I explored the different ways to rig aerial hammocks and the different styles of hammocks available for purchase. I even started looking into Aerial Yoga Teacher Training. I learned from anywhere I could! Even when looking at franchise options, I learned from their financial models and applied those learnings to my own business plan for a studio.

Then, I escaped my life and all my outside responsibilities to attend 7 days with Tony Robbins. Seven days of nothing but focus on me, my values, my beliefs and what I wanted for my life. My self-belief was the highest it had been in a long time and by the time I left that seminar, I knew that I needed to do whatever it might take to start my own Aerial Yoga studio.

The next day, I signed a lease on the studio space, scheduled Aerial Yoga Teacher Training in that new studio and started to look for other instructors to go on this adventure with me. I found when I set my mind and my heart in a direction, and with certainty in the positive outcome, something amazing occurred. Within one month, I had renovated the studio space, hired 14 instructors, set up the core operating system for the business, purchased everything necessary to make the business run, ordered my hammocks, got them hung and prepared for the studio to open. The most amazing life lesson through all of this was, when I had a clear focus the people and information I needed to help me achieve this goal wandered onto my path with perfect timing.

We opened our studio and taught our first classes in February of 2014. It was a sold out class, and so was every class for the months to follow. The local paper came to interview us and put our studio picture and information in a featured article on the front page of the Health and Wellness section. Who knew, I would go from being fired and feeling like I was unwanted, not enough, not worthy....to having an article written about my new business passion and our influence in the community?

Three short months and my entire life had changed dramatically! I went from an employee to business owner, from wearing an HR hat to wearing a marketing, sales, leadership, and training hats and from doing a role where my soul was not alive, to running a business built from the heart not the head. I loved every minute of the journey! Along the way, there were many bumps in the road and life lessons to learn. But as I look back on this journey, it wasn't only a journey for me. The decision to make my vision a reality positively impacted me, my family, my instructors, and our 2000 or more studio patrons. Some of those patrons tried our classes once or twice, and some were regulars who showed up 3 or more times per week. We taught adult and kids classes, singles and couples classes, physical asana and meditation classes, and many others along the way. But mostly, we created a safe place for people to wander in as they were going through their own life transitions. The transitions of college life, moving to a new place, losing a loved one, wanting to lose weight or grow muscle, wanting to find some friends.......our little studio created a nurturing community for like-minded people to feel safe as they grew their own wings. By giving meaning to idea that being fired wasn't something done TO ME, but rather something done FOR ME, I FOUND ME.

My Resiliency Lessons:

1. Challenge your beliefs – they may have served you at one time, but they may not be serving you now. My belief that Corporate America was the only secure way to make a living came crashing down on me. If I had not challenged that belief, I would not have opened my studio.

2. Get a new perspective – words and events are nothing more than the meaning we give them. Are you giving them a meaning that will help launch you forward, or are you giving them a meaning that will hold you back. If I had held onto the meaning of being fired as one that I was not enough, unwanted, or incapable, I would have been led to take a lower level role in another company. But since I changed the meaning to believe this was an opportunity for me to start a new journey, I was able to thrive in my new experience.

3. Push your comfort zone – in order to grow you need to take on new challenges and sometimes those are way outside your comfort zone. I took this to a bit of an extreme. Starting a business in an area where I had little experience and skill (aerial yoga) or even knowledge as a business owner made my growth curve a little steep, but it also increased my sense of accomplishment and my resolve that I can do anything I put my mind to.

4. It's all about the journey – everything in life is either growing or dying. As long as you are growing on your journey, you will feel alive. Be thankful for the journey and not just the outcome. I didn't know much about aerial yoga or running a business when I started this studio, but along the way I learned and some amazing individuals were placed in my path to help me gain the skills necessary.

5. Act with Grace, especially to yourself - you will make mistakes, but that is how we learn. Be easy on yourself and love yourself through it all. Show yourself and those around all the love you can muster and you will get that love and grace in return!

Rhonda Nichols has a BS in Retail Management and MS in Industrial Technology from Purdue University, but her true education has come from ALL the successes and ~~failures~~ learning opportunities along life's journey.

A native of Indiana, and a Texan for most of her adult life, Rhonda has weathered the joys and disappointments of being raised by a single mom (who is definitely her greatest role model and best friend) and two devoted grand-parents (both now her Angel guides), parenthood (of a son and a daughter that have 8 years between their births and are blessed with independent spirits), intimate loving relationships, life-long friendships, a career in Human Resources for high tech companies and currently in the financial services industry, and ownership in many entrepreneurial experiments.

As a life-long learner and avid personal development junkie, Rhonda has always felt she has a bigger purpose in life. After listening to her first Tony Robbins audio books, and attending two of his live events, she was inspired to figure out just what that purpose was; helping others through shifts and transitions in life.

She has had the opportunity to meet many fantastic women along this journey and realized that all of them had stories of learning and growth that needed to be shared. This book was her way to begin sharing those journeys in the hope that others will find solace in the similarities or have compassion for their differences to each author in this book. May this lead you to continue on your journey and find your purpose through your passion!

10

All Will Be Okay

L.I. Tibbets

I was sitting at a small table in the middle of a hole in the wall bar, drinking beers with my friend. Rachel was telling me about her divorce because she discovered her husband was having an affair. The year was 2012. I was about three years into my relationship with James. I remember telling her that if James ever broke up with me; I'd probably be hiding under my covers in the fetal position high on heroin for weeks. I couldn't imagine my life without him and absolutely did not want to. *James would never do that to me. Thank God I have such a great boyfriend who loves me. He would never cheat on me.*

Fast forward to 2015. I was just persistently anxious, uncomfortable, fat, and feeling ugly. I was constantly annoyed about something; work, school, James, my friends, and the list goes on. It was like every day was the worst day of my life.

Sunday, November 15, 2015 was an ideal fall day. Atypical for Indiana weather, the sun was shining and it was warm enough to be outside without a coat on. James sat on our couch in our living room and was doing homework because it was one of four days per month that he was off of work. I wanted so badly for him to spend time with me. I was trying so hard to be understanding that he needed to get his homework done. I occupied myself by catching up on household tasks, spending time in the warm weather outside, and thinking. However, per usual, my thinking turned to anxiousness and irritability: *If he managed his time better, he would have his homework done and could spend time with me. I work just as hard, if not harder, than he does and I also go to school part time. My job is extremely emotionally and mentally taxing. He must not really love me. If he did, he would make time to spend with me.* These thoughts became too much and I just had to speak my mind. Our conversation turned to an argument, which turned into a screaming match. I was out of control and upset at which point he said he would leave. I yelled, "MAYBE I SHOULD LEAVE!"

To which he replied, "Maybe you should leave and never come back!" Never in his life had he responded to my antics so quickly, calmly, or without hesitation. Normally he would take some time to think before he responded. I stormed into our bedroom closet and hovered over my dresser. I was in such a rage, slamming the dresser drawers. After hours of crying, I fell asleep.

I got up Monday morning still in the same rage, but with an added hint of shame. I showered, got ready for work, and saw James sleeping on our couch on my way out of the bedroom. After a few tries I managed to wake him up and asked, "Did you mean what you said?"

He didn't answer.

"Did you mean what you said when you said to leave and never come back?"

"Yeah."

And after a five-year relationship, that was it. I literally could not believe it. I was supposed to head to Chicago in 5 days, so I booked a hotel room until my trip. The upcoming Saturday, the sixth night, I was supposed to be in Chicago anyhow. I thought to myself, *this will show him. I will leave and be gone for a week. That will show him. He will not think I will actually leave. But when I don't show up at home today, or tomorrow, or for the next six days, THAT will show him.*

But James didn't reach out at all. He didn't ask where I was, he didn't ask how I was doing, he didn't call, and he didn't text; he didn't care. I stopped by our house one evening that week to get some clothes and do some laundry. I purposely went in the evening because I knew he would be at work. But he was there. He didn't talk to me. He still didn't ask where I was, how I was doing, he didn't call, and he didn't text; he still didn't care. That week in the hotel, I cried more than I had in the last five years combined.

I wrote in my journal, *"Now it's Saturday. You still haven't talked to me. I'm afraid it's real – it's over. But I still have hope that you've just had a super busy week, and that we haven't had an opportunity to really talk. Maybe you need time."*

My obligations in Chicago got cancelled so I texted him and said I would be coming to the house and he said that was fine. I asked him to hold me, and he did. I prayed that this wasn't the end. I gave him my body in hopes that my sexuality would keep him from leaving.

We spent Thanksgiving apart with our respective families. I kept everything to myself for fear of having to defend him when we got back together. I tried to put on a happy face while I choked on tears.

James had been planning to go out of town to see his cousins up north the weekend after Thanksgiving for several months. He even extended his trip. My hopes and plans of using my body to keep James tied to me didn't work. James had not changed his mind about breaking up. It was that moment that I knew it was over. I honestly don't really remember what happened after that. I turned to my journal again. *"I physically feel ill and I hurt. My heart is broken. I feel like a terrible, nasty, ugly person. Why would you be intimate with me after breaking up with me? Why did you kiss me two days ago? How do I move on? How do I go on? I'm not strong in that way like you are. I'm breaking down, I'm stressed out. I wonder down the road if you'll regret this and by then will it be too late? I just want you to hold me close, tell me you love me, and that everything will be okay."*

The morning after he left for his trip, I didn't know what to do with myself. I felt like I was crawling out of my skin. My first thoughts were to grab alcohol, drugs, or weapons but, thank God, instead I called my mom. I hadn't reached out to my mom for help for over eight years. I was desperate, alone, and it was a dark, dark place. After hanging up, I got down to business. I took down all of our pictures and started making a pile of my belongings in our bedroom. I moved my things into the guest bedroom and guest bathroom. All the while, I felt like I was literally losing my mind. I wondered, *what am I going to do?* I had my entire life planned out with this man and I had gotten rid of essentially all of my personal belongings seven months prior when he asked me to move into the house he purchased.

Even though I had to maintain my work responsibilities, I managed to find an apartment and signed a lease starting in December. One night after a large work event, I started moving everything I own all by myself in the "it's-so-cold-it-hurts" Indiana weather. I moved my belongings car load by car load until all that was left was what I physically could not move all by myself: bed, dresser, TV stand, desk, and headboard.

The support that I had during that time will stay with me for the rest of my life: my two best friends and my mom. Other friends stepped up to the plate as well and supported me in different ways (making me eat, dragging me to social events, taking me to the store). In my previously perpetually negative mindset, I did not know I had so many people who loved and cared about me. I didn't think I was deserving of such support. The experience was truly humbling to see who is there for you during such an extreme circumstance in life.

In the meantime, I also stopped getting so stressed about work. Prior to this huge life event, I was constantly worried about work tasks and responsibilities but I remember sitting at my desk, feeling like a zombie, and thinking, *there are WAY more important things in life than this job.*

I started to heal from my relationship with James. I realized that I didn't want to be with someone who didn't bother to check on me for a full week, even after our 5 year relationship. I realized what I need from a partner and also who I want to be in a relationship.

When February rolled around, things started to look up. My journaling continued, *"I have my own apartment now. It's like a little house. I am having so much fun. I am getting along with so many people and love spending time with people I never would have. I'm doing whatever I want and being who I want to be: nice, fun, funny, honest, real. And people like me for this. Multiple people tell me how much happier I seem and that's because I am...I look at things so differently now...what's the point of passing judgments on people? Life is too fucking short...I'm strong, independent, good-looking, funny, and a good person. I deserve to be with someone who appreciates all aspects of me."*

I had a new normal. I started functioning again: getting through the day without tears, choosing to spend time with my friends, and meeting new people. I realized I could actually "do life" without James. That's when I started feeling empowered because I was accomplishing life tasks on my own when just a few years ago I thought it was something I could never do alone. The more I focused on how empowered I felt; the more driven I was to overcome any life obstacles. I never thought I could be on my own because I relied on James for so many things, but I found I can actually do a lot more by myself than I ever thought possible! I've also learned through healthy relationships, that I am a good person and people like me, a lot. Other guys starting reaching out. Even though I thought James and I would get married, I was reminded there are other options out there.

I had a setback when James reached out to me on my birthday. He sent me a link to a funny YouTube video that we used to watch together. When he asked to see me, my vision blurred and I felt like I was in another universe. I agreed and felt excited. This was the first time seeing him in 7 months, and there he was standing in my living room holding my favorite cake. It was like a dream. We chatted about work and school and kept the conversation on the surface. It was comforting to be physically close to him. I cried when he left and wondered why he chose to reach out.

This opened up the doors of communication and we casually corresponded for the next month. I thought there was a chance that he wanted to get back together. I journaled again, *"I made the mistake for the millionth time in six years to get my hopes up for the first time in seven months and he fucking didn't follow through. It was so fucking simple."*

It was my journal that helped me the most. I read my past journal entries about how James made me feel over the past year. I didn't want to dwell in my sadness or disappointment again. He was not worth it. I had come too far forward and I would not go back.

Because of what I have been through and overcome, I have learned so much about myself and am confident in who I am. Hurdles will never go away. Whether the hurdle is a man, drugs, food, sex, and so forth. There will always be barriers or even complete catastrophes in life that will throw you for a loop. But that does not mean it's over and it doesn't mean it's worth giving up. It IS possible to get through circumstances that you would have never dreamed you could overcome.

LJ has a Bachelor's of Science degree in Youth, Adult, and Family Services and a minor in Psychology from Purdue University. She is currently earning her Master's in Social Work at Indiana University Purdue University – Indianapolis. LJ has worked in human services for over ten years in various capacities and has experience with a multitude of disadvantaged populations. Her human service work is founded in the strengths perspective and resiliency theory and she truly believes in people's abilities to overcome. She has used her professional experience to overcome obstacles in her personal life as well and is passionate about helping others do the same.

11

Perfect Chinese Princess

Angela Cheng

Chasing the Illusion of the Perfect Princess

Angst in the Early Years

I am sobbing, whimpering, cowering against the corner of our middle-class suburban kitchen in Toronto, Canada.

"Please don't hit me." I whimper, tears flowing down my cheeks. "Please don't hit me."

I am 13. I am the only daughter to strict Asian immigrant parents. I was raised to be a Perfect Chinese Princess. I tried really hard to meet that ideal. Some days, I thought I came close. Most days, I didn't think I could cut it. I never really felt sufficient, never felt good enough.

That morning when I was 13, I knew I had failed in meeting the ideal again. I was being made to drink this awful concoction of microwaved milk mixed with raw egg. You see, my parents thought I wasn't eating enough nutritious food, and they thought making me drink this would be good for me. It was part of an ongoing battle with my parents that I never won. I was punished when I didn't behave to their standards, in particular regarding what and how much food I should eat. As a young girl, I found myself dreading some mealtimes, especially if I knew I didn't feel like eating.

I looked at the microwaved milk and egg mixture and shook my head, trembling and starting to cry. My mom motioned to my dad to give out the typical punishment for disobedience. I was terrified. I knew what was about to happen.

My father took out the rolling pin from the kitchen drawer. As my dad swung towards my buttocks, I instinctively tried to block it with my hand, so he hit my hand instead of my buttocks. That strike broke my hand.

I lied to the doctor who treated me at the hospital. I told him I had fallen down the stairs and had got my hand caught in something.

After that, my father went down on his knees, cried in front of me and begged for my forgiveness. To both my parents' credit, they didn't hit me again after that. But the judgment and criticism continued - I still never felt sufficient enough to meet their standards. I never could reach the illusion of being the Perfect Princess.

Discipline or Abuse?

Was that experience an example of discipline, or abuse? To some, the answer may be obvious. For myself, I had trouble labelling my childhood experiences. I didn't like the word abuse – that always happened to other people, not to me. In fact, I avoided reflecting on the question until I was in my 40s, when I shared some of my traumatic childhood experiences with one of my best friends. She was a Chinese woman who grew up with me, and whose mother was one of my mom's best friends. When I told her that as a child I was hit if I didn't follow my parents' wishes – whether it be not citing the multiplication tables fast enough or not eating their food – she was aghast. She looked at me with a mixture of sorrow and anger. I had first thought she would defend my parents – that they loved me, that it was just discipline that I deserved. But that wasn't what she said. She said she was sorry she wasn't there to help me then, and that she had no idea that was happening under my roof. She said parents are supposed to take care of me, make sure I am fed, make sure I get a good education…but not to hit me if I didn't eat or meet their standards.

I ended up defending my parents more than my best friend defended them. I told her that my parents loved me, and that they were just judging and punishing me like their parents had did to them. That it was a Chinese custom passed down from generation to generation – they only wanted the best for their child - so why would I label that as abusive? Surely she understood, since she also had Chinese parents.

I remember her sighing and shaking her head, emphasizing that she was not hit as a child. And that parents are there to protect you, not to hit you.

That conversation with my best childhood friend was catalytic for me. I was compelled to re-visit and review my past. It's hard for me to find words to describe my childhood that captures its many different facets. I could say

162

I had a good, middle-class upbringing where my parents did their best to love me and provide for me. I could say that as an only daughter to immigrant parents, I felt a lot of pressure to live up to their high standards of what a 'good daughter' should be. I had plenty of loving childhood moments - my mom singing to me, my dad telling me childhood stories, my mom brushing my hair, my dad teaching me how to ride a bike. Fortunately, moments of pain and despair were not as frequent as the moments of gentleness. However, moments of despair created blunt imprints in my memory – my mom screaming at me and striking me for not reciting multiplication tables fast enough, my dad in a rage spanking me in front of my uncles as I wasn't eating at the dinner table. As a child I learned quickly to try to behave in a way that received acknowledgement and praise, but there always seemed to be an underlying threat of admonishment or punishment. My mom would say in a somewhat joking manner that she criticized those she loved most. Thus, judgment and criticism prevailed in our house, veiled in what I thought was love. The constant judgment against a perfect ideal meant I did not feel good enough in my own skin.

I reflected a lot on what abuse was. After doing some research and drawing from my own childhood experiences, I can offer this definition of abusive behaviour:

Abusive behaviour is an action that harms or reduces, often in a repetitive manner. Abusive behaviour includes anything that is designed to make you feel not whole, not complete, not sufficient or not good enough as you are.[2]

Abusive behaviours not only include physical, but also any behaviour that affects you on an emotional or mental level. So, even though my parents stopped physically hitting me when I was 13, the emotional/mental abuse continued in that there was a constant criticism and push for me to become that perfect ideal.

The Mind as the Abuser

Our minds can be our greatest abuser. You don't need to have experienced an abusive childhood, or have had abusive interactions with another, to know what abuse feels like. It's that persistent chatter in your head that you are not good enough. That somehow you are lacking in intelligence, looks, skills, or whatever else your mind can conjure.

What are some of the things your mind tells you that denigrate or abuse who you are?

---

[2] Definition is based on the series 'Abuse and Its Pleasures' by The Wonders

I have realized that our minds can be the worst and most constant abusers in our lives. The mind's nature is to strive for a perfection that can never be sustained or achieved.

My parents' example and patterns of judgment, control and perfection were instilled in me from early childhood. As a result, long after I left my parents' home and they no longer were present to criticize or judge me – I simply judged and criticized myself. I constantly held myself up against a perfect ideal that I could never achieve. I became my own best abuser. I rarely felt I was good enough. There was always something more I could do to be better.

I became a perfectionist and control freak in all areas of my life due to the constant judgment of my mind that I wasn't good enough. I looked happy enough on the outside, but inside I was miserable. I was so miserable constantly that I didn't even want to see it as miserable – it was just normal. I was comfortable with my own self-abuse. That subtle misery was all I knew…so I just smiled through it. Fake laughter came out of me. Life became a constant struggle, a never-ending cycle of self-judgment and stress. No matter what I tried, moments of happiness were at best fleeting, and I never seemed to be able to achieve and sustain true happiness and fulfilment.

Mastering the Inner Bully - Re-training the Mind

Shedding Victim Mentality

A key part of my healing from abuse came from realizing that even though someone may demonstrate *abusive behaviour* towards you, it does not mean you are an *abuse victim*. It dawned on me that even though I experienced abusive behaviour as a child, I didn't need to define myself by it. My healing process included taking back my power, and seeing that I was whole, complete, sufficient, and good enough as I am. I quieted and re-trained the critical voices in my mind…what I term 'mastering my inner bully'. I became strong through my healing process. I learned to forgive myself. I learned to forgive the little girl who believed she wasn't good enough as she was. Through that strengthening, healing and self-forgiveness process, I learned to forgive my parents. I could then see, through loving eyes, that my parents did do the best they could. To them, loving did and still does equate to judging, controlling and criticizing. I learned that truly loving them means allowing their choices and behaviours. Allowing their abusive behaviours does not mean that I condone their behaviour, it just means that my role becomes setting loving boundaries for myself and to limit my interactions with them, especially when they display abusive behaviours.

166

Thus, irrespective of abusive behaviours that are thrown your way, you are not an abuse victim if you know yourself to be good enough as you are. Once you know your wholeness, completeness, and sufficiency, rather than succumb to feeling like a victim when abuse occurs, you could then set boundaries and limit interactions with those who demonstrate abusive behaviours.

Igniting my 'Fire in my Belly'

When I was 16, I felt depressed. My constant feeling of not being good enough was omnipresent. I thought, there must be something more than *this*. To get myself out of my funk, I began to read. Much of what I read explored self-growth and spirituality. I remember reading a book called *'Many Lives, Many Masters'* by Dr. Brian Weiss. That book opened up a new world for me in that it helped me begin to see that I was more than just a physical body that aged and died. I began to realize and uncover my spirit. And that ignited a fire in my belly to continue to explore and uncover who I was. If I hadn't ignited my desire to explore and grow, it was likely I would have eventually committed suicide. This 'fire in the belly' drive for exploration and self-empowerment carried me through the rest of my teenage years, and gratefully still burns brightly in me to this day.

Being My Own Best Friend

Never feeling that I was good enough meant primary relationships were difficult for me. I didn't feel confident dating, so I didn't have my first boyfriend until I was 17. I attracted men who didn't truly love me, and I didn't truly love them…because I didn't love myself. I've lived through a failed marriage and several failed relationships. I spent a lot of time being single – about 7 years during my 20s, and again about 7 years during my late 30s and 40s. The time being single was priceless for me because each time I learned to like myself more and not to depend on another to make me happy.

In that time alone I learned to like myself, and then to learn to love myself. I taught my mind to be less judgmental, controlling and perfectionist. In that process, I chose to transform from being miserable to being happy, regardless of the circumstances.

I often travelled on my own. I remember I was renting a place in Pismo Beach, California. The place I rented happened to be a beautiful large master suite built for couples, and it had a breathtaking view of the water and sunset. No one – not even close family or friends - knew I was there. I was alone. And yet I didn't feel alone, and I knew I never would be alone. It was in that moment I knew I was my own best friend.

I'm dating again, and still learning. As my need for a perfect partner fades, I am ready to just live my life and allow someone to come into my life when the moment presents itself. Until then, I am happy being my own best friend.

Creating Magic in Workplaces

My perfectionist attitudes towards myself and others spilled over to my workplaces. I've been a management consultant for over two decades. In the beginning, I was a total control freak. Not only did I want to be seen as perfect, I wanted everyone else to follow my exacting standards. I was truly a micro-manager. My turning point was when I realized one team member lied to me and knowingly went against my authority. He did this because I wouldn't listen to his ideas, as I was being too rigid and controlling about his work. He and other team members didn't feel valued or respected. I had created a toxic team environment rather than one that was truly productive and naturally creative and expansive.

As I grew to like and love myself more, and in letting go of my perfectionist goals for myself and others, my workplaces and teams shifted. I created a training program for the work environment teaching employees and teams practical tools for fostering respect and self-love within the workplace. All aimed to reduce stress and drama and to increase efficiency and productivity. I am now a respected management consultant, and one of the qualities I'm appreciated for is creating 'magic' in helping individuals and teams work together in achieving goals.

Becoming Diet-Free

My striving to be a Perfect Chinese Princess meant I had to look perfect – have that slim, Asian perfect model-like figure. In my early 20s, I felt so insufficient that I experienced a few months of bulimia and anorexia. I remember eating a few grains of rice for dinner. I recall counting every calorie and throwing up after meals I deemed as 'bad'.   It's taken me a couple of decades to find my balance and to love my body. I have found that in removing judgment of my body and removing the *need* to have a slim body – I can then *choose* to be healthy and be slim. A radical new non-diet – a lifestyle where I'm not constantly battling my own body. I honour my body, nourish it, and because of the growth in my self-love, don't choose to over-eat and purge in a vicious cycle. Because I love and trust my body more now, my body can naturally stay slim and healthy and I get to enjoy and love food!

Letting Go of the Perfect Princess

Honest Self-Assessment

Before I could let go of my perfectionist and controlling attitudes and behaviours, I had to honestly assess where I was at first. The following are some questions that helped me in my journey, and may help you in yours.

1. Do you judge yourself and find yourself lacking – e.g. looks, weight, skills, intelligence, etc.?
2. Do you seem to be attracting stressful, drama-filled relationships and/or work environments?
3. To you, are things usually clearly right or wrong, good or bad, black or white?
4. How rigid are you in your daily/weekly routines?
5. How rigid are you in how life should be and ought to be?
6. How often do you use these words - 'must', 'should', 'could', 'would'?
7. Are you driven with the thought that you *must* succeed?
8. Do you view your life as having some fleeting moments of success, but the rest of the time you see yourself as 'just not making it' yet?
9. Do you feel compelled to plan out your life and its related projects, and spend much of your time making sure every last detail is perfect?
10. Are you a micro-manager?

11. How often do you feel stressed, frustrated and/or angry?
12. How often do you feel depressed?
13. Do you find your mind constantly obsessing over things?
14. What is your primary reaction to change – is there much resistance and fear?
15. Do you sometimes feel like you are on a hamster wheel – doing the same things over and over again, yet hoping for different results?
16. Do you feel that you are constantly juggling multiple balls in the air and are in fear that something will fall?
17. Do you feel that you are constantly pushing and striving in all or parts of your life?
18. Do you sometimes feel you are at war with yourself? Battling your body/weight? Battling your mental attitudes? Battling your emotions?
19. Answer these honestly while looking at yourself in the mirror – do you like yourself? Do you love yourself?
20. Are you truly, underneath it all, happy with your life?

These questions can help shed some light on any perfectionist and controlling attitudes and behaviours you may have. But please don't pass judgment on yourself if you are or have experienced any or all of the above! I personally have experienced some form of all of them. And it's ok to not be ready to change – I know I resisted change for a long while, as control and perfection were all I knew. I was so busy 'perfecting' my perfectionist behaviours that I didn't want to stop, and I didn't want to let go. It wasn't until there were times I felt completely overwhelmed that I knew I had to make some changes to how I lived my life. So, I would recommend to just be honest with yourself as to whether you are ready to change, and what you are ready to change. If and when you've had enough, if you choose, I can help you to let go and add more ease and fulfilment to your life.

The 'Perfect Life'

I was, am, and always will be a *recovering* perfectionist and control freak. I view it as a life-long journey, and one that I find extremely fulfilling as I continue moving forward. In the past 20 years, I have spent on average one week per month in an intense program of exploration, expansion and empowerment. This was instrumental in helping me through much of my perfectionist and controlling attitudes and behaviours. And the benefits are truly priceless. I like me, I love me, and I am happy. Ironically, I see myself with a 'Perfect Life'. As in, everything is perfect, *just as it is*.

I Am Sufficient

What would I say to my 13-year old self, cowering in the middle-class suburban kitchen, so fearful that she was not good enough and thus must be punished? I would tell her that she is OK. That she doesn't need to strive to be that

Perfect Chinese Princess. That she is good enough, whole, complete, sufficient – just as she is.

I hope that you find in yourself that you are good enough, whole, complete, sufficient, just as you are.

Greetings!

I am passionate about helping people to be happy and in love...with themselves. As a recovering perfectionist and control freak, I offer practical tips and guidance in experiencing a more fulfilling, ease-filled and productive life. I reach people through professional speaking, coaching, and management consulting.

As a child, I was raised in a strict, abusive environment which encouraged me to become a "Perfect Chinese Princess" rather than to embrace who I really was. I hung on to perfection and control as my main tools, and as a result I didn't realize until later in my life just how abusive I had become, both to myself and others. My recovery from that, to become my happy, authentic self, is a journey I like to help others to take.

An integral part of self-love is understanding the difference between discipline and abuse, especially self-abuse. I bring awareness to the mind's tendency to act as an 'inner bully' in that it can be focused on achieving a perfection and ultimate control that is illusory, and ultimately harmful to the self.

I help individuals to transform and quiet the mind, so that our minds can become an ally rather than a contractive force in our lives.

As a result of a fierce 'fire in the belly' passion for expansion and self-empowerment, for the past 20 years I have spent a week per month studying with The Wonders. I have chosen to be part of an intense life-long program, and as a result I have become a Certified Teacher of The Wonders, which means I walk my talk about experiencing more love and ease, and can help you to do the same.

With love,
Angela Cheng

#LoveYourselfMore #MasterInnerBully
#DisciplineVsAbuse #RecoveringPerfectionist #PerfectLife
#IAmSufficient
http://Angela.Global

12

Living For The Next Day

Amberly Simpson

I lay there completely collapsed on the concrete slab that was our porch, whaling and sobbing uncontrollably. It was late June of 2014 and I was supposed to be on my way to take the GRE right now at a testing facility, but instead Nathan, my husband, was picking me up off the floor and supporting the weight of my body as we stumbled down the lawn toward his car. He put me in the passenger seat, shut the door, and got in on the driver's side to take me to my test before it was too late.

"I don't want to live anymore," I sobbed over and over again as we drove. "I have nothing to live for." I was inconsolable.

Nathan didn't respond to anything I was saying, he just drove. When we arrived at the testing facility, a Sylvan Learning Center, he got me out of the car, sent me inside, and left. I cried silently the entire time I was taking the test, though I somehow pulled off a strong and high-performing score. Several hours later, when it was all over, he was there again; we sat in silence the entire drive home. I had thoroughly exhausted myself from the hysterics at this point, but everything around me was still a blur of a life that I was stuck living.

This was the lowest point of my life to date. The point where I, someone who prided myself on my positivity, optimism, and a genuine love of life, found myself so deeply trapped within an abusive relationship that I was ready to end my life.

I remember the day I met Nathan. I was going into my fourth year of undergrad at Purdue, my second year dancing for the Purdue Contemporary Dance Company, and he had showed up for the audition. He was a natural mover. Not necessarily a strong technical dancer, but someone who just had their own unique movement style and really knew how to make it shine on stage. I remember watching him move at the audition and specifically singling him out to work with my friend Anna on a particular lift. I was drawn to him innately.

Nathan ended up being cast in the same dance piece as me, so we started to see each other more and to hang out, at first circumstantially, but more deliberately as time went on. We would text or call each other randomly and we started going on long walks around Purdue's campus, talking and meandering for hours. It turned out that our birthdays fell back to back, mine being the fourth of September and his being the fifth. He brought me a watermelon, my favorite fruit, as a gift, a gesture I found simple but profoundly observant and meaningful. We also both loved literature and would spend time taking turns reading to each other from various books.

Eventually, our conversations stopped being on campus and started moving to each other's houses. One night I fell asleep on Nathan's couch after we had made dinner. He was a perfect gentleman; he left me there and went to sleep in his own bed, leaving a thin blanket behind for me. Despite this, I woke up in the middle of the night freezing cold and half asleep, so I found him in his room and asked if I could join him. As suspicious as it sounds, I truly had every intention of just falling asleep in a warmer environment and calling it at that. Perhaps he did too. But lying in bed together became the accidental bumping of limbs. Bumping became lingering, and lingering became the gradual slide into each other like puzzle pieces. I was fully awake now. We giggled and talked quietly, gently and playfully biting each other on the nose, ear, neck, cheek. And then at once I was biting his lip, not even realizing that I was actually kissing him softly, warmly. To my surprise, he was kissing me back. This was the moment everything stopped being simple.

It wasn't until after I was out of it that I was able to see how abusive my relationship with Nathan had been. It happens gradually and you are slowly manipulated so that you learn to think about the relationship the way the abuser wants you think about it. You learn to trust their words over your own, to isolate yourself so no other opinions can penetrate your relationship or be heard. If you're not careful, you will lose yourself entirely, which, if they have done their job as craftily as Nathan did, you won't even notice it's happening at all.

It wasn't even a year later that Nathan I were married, and while any logical person could see the dangers and risks with this, I was swept away into him, already partly lost to his way of thinking. It all happened in a whirlwind and blur where the love was instantaneous and easy. He inspired me, he frightened me. It was easy to ignore the lows when the highs were so intense and full of passion. Even as the highs became slowly and increasingly outnumbered by the lows, you learn to crave and only see the potential of those highs, even when you find they are almost non-existent anymore. All of you exists in those highs. Thus, when it came to leaving the relationship, to say the least, I got lucky. I would love to say that I displayed some incredible show of bravery or understanding, but the reality is that my ability to leave can be traced back to four happy circumstances that provided me with tools and awareness I needed at the exact right moments.

The first of these tools was the combination of having a confidant and the ability to see alternatives. I knew that I was unhappy and that things were not stable or healthy, but I was under a deeply held belief that had been trained into me that these things were my fault, that I wasn't being good enough to the relationship, that I was failing and I just needed to work harder to make things successful. By whatever strike of chance or luck, around the time that things were starting to go downhill at their fastest, I was contacted by an old friend of mine from high school named David. Conveniently enough, he had contacted me only a few days before I went on a road trip to visit some friends in North Carolina one weekend, so we agreed to catch up while I was driving.

David and I spent the entirety of the drive both to and from North Carolina on the phone with each other, and in the process of this, he became the first person I could open up to about what I was experiencing in my relationship.

It started out first as catching up; we hadn't spoken to each other in about four years, so there was a lot to talk about. We shared what we had been doing in college over the past few years, the travels and adventures we had taken, funny stories, difficult stories. It was a rush of joy from the past. But when all of that ran out, there was still the elephant in the room: Surprise! I was married and things weren't exactly going well.

David didn't outright tell me that there was anything wrong with the way that I was being treated, but he was a listening ear. In fact, he was the first listening ear that I'd had in several months since I had started being isolated from my other relationships. I saw David as safe in a way that my other friends were not because there was no way that our verbal conversation could get back to Nathan. So I spilled. I spilled how I had to keep a nine-digit passcode on my phone to keep Nathan from going through all my accounts and messages, how he would scream at me, how he had kicked an 18" diameter hole in our wall from one room to the next in anger at me for talking with a male friend, how he wouldn't let me talk to my other friends, how my male friends were all supposedly trying to get me into bed with them. I put it all out on the table and David just listened, took it in, allowed me to put my distress out there and let it exist somewhere other than in my head. It was the first safe space I'd had in months, my only safe space now.

However, things changed on the drive back from North Carolina when we were talking as usual and David stopped me:

"Amberly, I need to talk to you about something and I need you to just listen until I'm done. Can you do that?" I could. "I have been in love with you since high school. I didn't think those feelings would come back the way that they did, but...I want to be with you. I could give you a better life than what you have now and we could be happy together. You told me so many things about taking chances in high school and how we regret the chances we don't take more than the ones we do. I have nothing to lose, but I'll always remember not having told you how I feel if I don't"

I was dumbfounded...sort of. In high school, David and I had briefly had feelings for each other, but they never came into fruition, instead, being long-replaced with sincerity and contentment. Our relationship had always been one of friendship. Talking to him now, those feelings somewhat came rushing back, but so many years later and given the situation that I was in, it wasn't more than a feeling of nostalgia and innocence, perhaps the kind you feel when you think back on a first love or an old friend whom you love unconditionally. With where I was in life, I couldn't even fathom the idea of a relationship with anyone else, let alone this blast from the past.

"I can give you a better life," he told me over and over again. "You don't have to live this way. If you come with me, things can be better for you."

"David, it's not that simple," I tried to tell him. "I'm married. I can't just walk away. It's not that I don't like and care for you, but I'm stuck in a pretty serious commitment. There's a lot I'd have to do to walk away from that, I couldn't just up and leave." This was the first time I had acknowledged to myself that I didn't have to be in my marriage. This was the first time I'd realized there were alternatives out there, other paths I could take. I had the option of walking away.

David and I dropped the topic from then on out. He never asked me to leave again, but we continued to talk for a few more days before something even more profound happened: David walked away. Out of nowhere he stopped answering texts, phone calls, or any other form of communication. To protect his heart, he left what he knew was going to be a toxic situation for him.

It was painful to not have him around anymore. I had finally found someone that I could confide in and then it disappeared. In the short term, this set me back tremendously, but in the long run David did exactly what he needed to, not only for himself, but for me. He showed me that I had not lost my freedom to choose whether that choice was to love or to leave.

Of course, it would be several months before this ever fully made sense to me, and in that time my relationship got progressively more abusive. I moved into a deeper state of depression that ultimately landed me to the state that started off this story. It was in one of those fits of suicidal hysteria that the second lesson I needed to learn came my way.

In the absence of a confidant, I turned to my mother for solace. One day, after I had taken the GRE, Nathan and I had gotten in another fight where he stormed out of the house for dramatic and manipulative effect and left me sobbing inconsolably at our kitchen table. I had no idea what to do. I felt like the only option for me was to end my life, but I knew somewhere inside myself that this was not what I had wanted. So I called my mother and told her what had happened in our latest fight, the things he had been saying to me, that I was just using him for his money, that my male friends didn't actually care about me, they "just wanted to fuck [me]" and were only sticking around for their moment to pounce. He'd also told me at this point that he was refusing to go with me anymore on our trip to California and Washington in order to visit my family.

When I told my mom about all of this, it was not only a shock to her because I had seemed to happy when she had visited months earlier, but she was outraged at his behavior. Regardless, I defended him. Even though I was the one calling because I didn't know what to do about how he was treating me, I defended him to the bone. I wanted to give him to benefit of the doubt because that's what had been trained into me. He must have been right.

Rather than telling me to leave or telling me he was a pig or an ass or completely delusional (which, of course, she made sure to make clear to me later), my mom gave me some simple tips for how to fight more fairly with him. The first thing was that we needed to not yell, swear, and get angry during our arguments, but try and keep things neutral. When you do this, it allows you to listen to what the person is actually saying rather than getting caught up in your emotions which tend to just escalate the situation as a whole. This was easier said than done, but I made a very active effort to do this. Most of the time I was successful, but sometimes I would still get angry or upset. What I started to notice was that Nathan also noticed when I did this. I would ask him to please not yell and to be civil as we talk to each other.

"Stop micromanaging my emotions," he would yell. Ultimately, it was clear that he was not going to prescribe to these rules of arguing. While that made it very difficult for me to keep a level head, especially given that I was not mentally healthy at the time, it did allow me to gain awareness of how I was being talked to and treated in a way that I couldn't see before when I, too, was wrapped up in anger, emotions, and yelling.

The second recommendation that my mother made was to only speak in "I" statements, especially when I was trying to confront his actions or the way he spoke to me. Supposedly, this was going to help make it more about my experience and less focused on how he was making me feel. I believe that, for a normal, healthy relationship this would be true at least most of the time, but in the presence of an abuser who would actively manipulate my words, it didn't seem to make a difference. That is, it didn't make a difference for him. What it did for me was bring my attention to my word choice. By putting myself at the center of how I was feeling, it gave me the opportunity to regain control of myself in our arguments. When he would try and twist what I was saying into an affront of him, I could redirect him back to what I had specifically said. By being more conscious of what I was saying, it was much harder to manipulate my words. This didn't necessarily stop him from doing so, but, again, awareness of what was going on was the primary thing that was lacking in my life because I had been trained to think how he wanted me to think.

Eventually the time came for me to go on the trip to visit my family that Nathan and I had planned. While I was still deeply hurt that I would now have to take a family trip alone, this also opened me up to the final two experiences I needed that empowered me to leave the relationship: an objective person who was blunt with me about what I was experiencing, and ample time away from Nathan's control and monitoring.

In Nathan's absence, my mother arranged for me to go and get some outside counseling. So a few days after arriving in

California, I met with a therapist and unloaded all of the things that had been going on: the yelling, the name calling, the sexualizing of my body and my relationships, the physical intimidation.

"He sounds abusive," the therapist told me flat out.

"No, he's definitely not. I know I'm painting it to seem that way, but I also owe him the benefit of the doubt," I responded.

"Why are you defending him?"

"I'm not defending him! I'm just trying to see it from his side. I'm trying to be as fair as possible so that I can see the relationship clearly. Like how he always says I'm micromanaging his emotions when I try and get him to calm down. That's legitimately how he feels so I owe him the benefit of trying to understand that and accommodate to it."

"He sounds like he's being abusive toward you."

The conversation circled with me defending him and the counselor telling me those actions and words were abusive, like this for about an hour and a half. The woman even went overtime on our session trying to get me to see what she was talking about, but I didn't. I couldn't! He wanted me to see him as right and after months and months of training to think that way, constantly being berated when I disagreed until I finally broke, It was all I could see anymore. The therapist even gave me several recommendations for books and movies to look into to help me see the parallels between my relationship and other abusive relationships. I didn't even pay them attention because I felt like she was so off-base. I stuffed them into my wallet without any intention of looking at them again and they eventually were lost or thrown away.

Nonetheless, hearing this was critical in providing me with the strength I needed to leave the relationship. I didn't need to see what she was talking about at that point in time, but what I did need was for someone to plant the seed. No matter what kind of denial I was in, there was still a part of me listening (likely the deeply miserable part that wanted to be happy again and somehow knew, albeit blindly, that it was possible). So when I started moving forward with these next few weeks without Nathan's ever-monitoring eye, without his manipulation of my thoughts, I started slowly seeing some of the things that the therapist was talking about. It didn't come in the form of outright insight; it was more subtle than that. It came in little things like happiness and enjoyment when spending time with my family. It came with the joy of hanging out with my friends from high school, the first I'd ever really gotten to spend time with friends in several months. It came from finally being able to open up to people about how unhappy I was, which was also the first I'd ever really admitted it to myself. It came from being able to go out with my dad and brother to a bar and just talk casually with people I didn't even know without being afraid of being seen talking to another person. It came in the form of having wonderful, warming conversations with everyone around me, while, at the same time, leaving every phone call with Nathan feeling like my life was worthless. It came the day before I flew back to Purdue when Nathan refused to pick me up from the O'Hare airport and I was left with no way home from Chicago. It came in reaching out to a friend whom I'd previously stopped talking to because of Nathan and his casual, happy willingness to pick me up when I was stranded in Chicago. It came in so many minor, seemingly insignificant gestures and interactions. By the end of the few weeks I had spent on my own, I knew, not just unconsciously, that I had to leave. I had actually admitted it to myself at this point in time and, while I wasn't thoroughly committed to it yet, this newly-discovered ability to see outside of the relationship was something that I couldn't unsee. This was when I really found my freedom: when my mind was set free. Anything that I could think, now, I could create.

Of course, it wasn't that simple. It never is. It took another month before I was actually able to leave, and I wouldn't honestly say that I technically left either. I think Nathan knew that I was different when I came back. I really stuck to the things I had learned and refused to get angry during any discussion, this time with much more success than I had found previously. So when he finally went the route of of threatening to leave me, I didn't protest. I just said "okay." He pulled out all the usual stops, storming out of the house, storming back in again multiple times, more yelling, accusations, and berating. Eventually he left for real and went down to his parents' place for the night. All I had to do until then was keep my silence, keep saying "okay" so that I wouldn't do what the pain in my heart was telling me to do: take him back. I knew that if I didn't leave now, I couldn't leave. I knew that I had to stick with it or it was going to kill me eventually as it almost had a few months earlier.

Once he was out of the house and gone for real, a moment of panic struck. How was I going to survive without him? He was all I knew! He *was* me. But then I took a deep breath and I called my friend Rachel. I spent several hours hanging out with her, filling her in on what had happened, but the moment I remember most distinctly was stepping out of the car to go and meet her at her place and feeling the uncontrollable desire to just run. So I did. I ran down the block at 2am laughing and giggling to myself, spinning on the sidewalk. I could feel air in my lungs in a way that I hadn't felt in over a year. I was free.

This euphoric feeling of freedom didn't last long. It lasted almost two weeks exactly before the reality of the loss set in. Nathan continued to try to get us back together, taking me to a counseling session with him, agreeing to change or do whatever I needed. He wasn't in it to be better, he just wanted to possess me; the therapist told me this privately after one of our sessions. We were still living in the same house, though sleeping in separate beds. I was still madly in love with him, and that hurt even worse because my identity was almost entirely attached to him. Segregating myself from that was excruciating, so much so that we almost got back together and agreed to give it another try after two and a half months of not being together. The downfall of that was, at that point, I had seen and understood too much. I had figured out that he was abusive at this point, and I'd seen what the original therapist in California had been talking about. I was too afraid to go back., and all of this was proven to me when, in November of 2014, after falling asleep on a movie, he broke into my phone again. I knew things truly would never change, so I ended it right then and there. For real this time. He left officially and moved in with his parents, leaving me the house to myself with both our belongings inside.

All in all, it was over a year later before I felt like myself again. Rather, it was over a year before I felt like I understood who I was now without the relationship. I went through several months of depression because I couldn't make sense of my self-concept. I had lost my identity entirely and I didn't know if I was the good, human person I had once thought I was; that was ambitious, worked her hardest and wanted to do her best to contribute to the world, or if I was the sex object and heathen that he had made me believe that I was. I oscillated between the two in my actions, trying them on to see which fit. Over time the oscillations became less extreme, but the question still remained.

Ultimately, what allowed me to let go of those final questions was the last day I saw him. I had signed our divorce papers in January of 2015, but we both finished moving our stuff out of the house in June. It was the first I had spoken to him face to face in almost eight months. I had graduated now and was preparing to leave Purdue in a few months. Even then, I was so terrified of him, I made my friend Will hide out in the house with me just to make sure I was okay.

The conversation between Nathan and me was cordial. He had nothing but good things to say and I was reminded of why I had fallen in love with him in the first place. It tugged on heart strings I didn't realize were left hanging, even though the interaction only lasted about 30 minutes. In the end, we agreed to go to lunch or dinner sometime to get caught up, but I knew it would never happen. I had no intention of going through with it and neither did he.

After Nathan left, I collapsed against one of the walls of the house and began sobbing. After a couple minutes of me crying, my friend Will came out of his hiding spot and sat down next to me.

"I'm sorry," I apologized. "I don't know why that was so difficult for me. Just the weight of everything that happened all came back." He paused and listened to me for a minute.

"You know," he told me. "You sounded very strong when you were talking to him just now."

When we think of resiliency, we often think of it in terms of deliberate, calculated actions and shows of mental strength that demonstrate our willingness to fight for ourselves and our goals. Sometimes it comes in this form, but I find that this view can also be twisted by hindsight bias. Much of the time when we fight, we are fighting blindly. We don't know what exactly we're fighting for at the time, and we may not even know why exactly we're fighting at all. Resiliency is stubborn in this way. It is sprinkled with luck and helping hands we sometimes forget to acknowledge played a pivotal role in our success. I will always carry scars from the time of my life that was spent with Nathan, but I am eternally grateful that, because of my own stubbornness and because of the people in my life, those things have become scars instead of open or fatal wounds. Are we always made to be stronger for our pain and suffering that we overcome? It's debatable. But what is always true is that we lived another day to be able to decide that for ourselves.

Amberly M Simpson was born and raised in Glendale, California where she grew up immersed in the arts. Her mother being an ex-ballet dancer, and her father a musician, she studied everything from piano to figure skating to theatre and singing recreationally, though dance was her primary passion.

In 2010, Amberly moved away from California to study at Purdue University, determined to get a career in Wildlife Biology and quit dance altogether. But, try as she might, dance was as inevitable to her life as breathing. After a one year hiatus, Amberly returned to dance with renewed and unbounded energy, this time focusing her studies on modern and ballet techniques, improvisation, nontraditional partnering, and pole dance techniques under the pseudonym Gatsby. She went on to dance for the Purdue Contemporary Dance Company for three years, choreographing for them twice, as well as found and direct a small aerial dance collective called UPROAR. Several of her works have also appeared in Purdue Dance Department's student concert, X Works, the American Dance Festival's 2013 Student Concert, the American College Dance Association's 2015 Central Conference, and with Obsessive-Compulsive Dance where she co-directed their summer concert in 2014. She has also had the honor of performing for TED Talks (2013, 2015), the Prague Quadrennial (2015), Voices HEaRD Kentucky (2017), and the Churchill Downs Fund for the Arts (2017). Beyond her dance credits, Amberly has had several creative writing pieces published, including poems, short stories, and creative nonfiction, in the Purdue Literary Magazine, *The Bell Tower*.

After five years studying at Purdue, Amberly graduated with honors in May of 2015 with dual degrees in Psychological Sciences and Creative Writing, as well as a minor in Dance. All of these areas of study have worked together to inform her creative works as well as offer new avenues for conceptual exploration within movement, writing, and education. Post-graduation, Amberly has danced for Blackbird Dance Theatre in Lexington, Kentucky (2015-2016), and is now a choreographer and performer for Suspend Performing Arts in Louisville, Kentucky (2016-present). Additionally, she is obtaining her Masters degree in Teaching at Bellarmine University and is currently an English Teacher in Louisville, Kentucky. She hopes to one day start her own dance company that creates works centered around social activism and performance as well as to continue her work as a writer of poetry, fiction, and creative nonfiction.

13

Hope Offers Forgiveness

Marie Kiana

Life was good in the very, very beginning. I was born in Hawaii and life was good! Then came the day my dad cheated on my mom and all hell broke loose. They fought horrendously for 6 months until my dad decided to leave my mom, my brother, and me and move to California. He chose to be with the woman he had been having an affair with. When he left, we watched my mom have a total breakdown.

She picked herself up and had a brief love affair but he wouldn't commit so, she decided to move to Australia to work at the US Embassy. She shipped my brother and me off to live with my dad, the woman, and her two kids. I was 6, Laurie was 7, my brother was 8,and Lem was 9.

Laurie and Lem weren't happy because they had to share their bedrooms with us. My brother and I weren't happy moving in with strangers. It was quite an adjustment for everyone going to a family of 6 overnight. I can remember so clearly all four kids shoved in the back seat of our Pontiac Monte Carlo. We got yelled at constantly and to keep us in line my dad started whipping us with a belt on our bare butts. What's worse is that if one of the kids did something wrong and didn't own up to it, we all got marched downstairs, to wait outside of his bedroom door while he whipped us one by one. The waiting was almost as bad as the whipping. I got whipped a lot.

We lived in California for almost a year, and we were going to move to Australia to live with my mom again. We were so excited! The day before we were supposed to go, my dad sat us down and said we weren't going because my mom was getting married. We were crushed, but a couple of months later we were able to move back to live with our mom, just in Hawaii instead of Australia. And not just my mom, but her new husband, my stepdad Bob.

We lived on Hickam Air Force Base, and life seemed pretty normal at first. Bob was really nice to us. He held my hand and paid a lot of attention to me. He was the affectionate, attentive Father I didn't have. He called me his special girl, and I felt like it. I really liked our new family.

I used to climb in bed with my mom and Bob on Saturday and Sunday mornings. My mom liked me to rub her feet while she read a magazine and Bob slept while the tv was on. Bob would ask me to rub his back, and when I was done, I'd lay down between them and watch tv. After a few times, he would take my hand and start rubbing his body with it. He would rub his shorts too. I didn't know better. My mom was right next to us. This started happening more frequently. Then Bob started tucking me in at night and whispering in my ear, "you are my special girl." I was too. He would watch me play and give me a lot of extra attention.   Then the attention turned to secrets. He started climbing in bed with me to tuck me in. I thought it was just like lying in my Mom's bed although he started kissing me good night more than just once and they lasted longer. He also would take my hand, and he would rub it on his shirt, then his arm, then his leg and land on his boxer shorts. Bob continued to tuck me in only he didn't just do it at bedtime, he started visiting in the middle of the night, and he no longer had my hand just rubbing his boxer shorts. There was a hole in the shorts and he started touching my body too.

We got transferred to Zaragoza Spain when I was 7. While staying on base in temporary housing; we had two bedrooms joined by a bathroom. My brother and I had bunk beds in our room, he insisted on sleeping on the top. One night, in the middle of the night, I awoke to my covers being pulled down and a finger on my lips and my panties being pulled off. The shame of what was happening to me and the fear my brother was going to wake up and see it was overwhelming. I froze and just pretended to be asleep. That was the worst night of my life and the moment that I was permanently scarred with shame.

The visits in the middle of the night kept happening over the next few years. Out of fear and a need to disappear, I kept pretending to be asleep. He kept telling me, "You are my special girl, and this is our secret: you can't tell anyone." Around the same time, my brother started to change. He started pushing me around, calling me names and doing things to hurt me intentionally. That's about the same time I started sleep walking and talking. I would go to bed and wake up in another part of the house. That went on for a while until one night I woke up sitting on the window ledge on the 3rd floor. I had my legs dangling out the window, and when I woke up, opened my eyes and looked down, I started screaming! Both Mom and Bob flew into the room and pulled me back inside. After that, my mom made the decision to send us back to live with my dad in California. I was ten.

California was easy because there was no Bob and my brother had my two step-siblings to pick on. I did sleep walk there too and would wake up in the middle of the night and not know where I was. I even slept walked to the boy's room next door and climbed to the 2nd story bunk and got in bed with my brother. My brother started yelling at me, and my dad ran in and flipped on the light. There I was on the top bunk with no idea of how I got there. I would also wake up screaming from nightmares. It went on for a while. My dad sent me to a psychologist, but I was too ashamed to let anyone know what happened with Bob. My brother went from hurting me to hurting animals. He pushed one of the cats off a 2nd story balcony, and he tied a string so tight around the other cat's foot that it almost had to be amputated. I got off easy that year. Although, there was one traumatic event that I will never forget. He stuck me in a rollaway bed and locked the top so I couldn't move my arms or legs. I couldn't move at all. Then, knowing my fear of the dark, he rolled it in the closet under the stairs and turned off the light. He left me in the pitch black unable to move for 3 hours. I've been claustrophobic ever since.

After a year in California, we rejoined my mom and Bob in Spain and moved to Germany; I was eleven. Bob would come in my room in the middle of the night. I was so afraid to go to sleep I would ask my mom if I could sleep on their floor. Sometimes she would let me. I told my mom that I don't want to be alone with him because he touches me. She asked where and I pointed to my private parts and she said, "no, you are just misunderstanding him, he loves you" and told me to go get changed.

Both my mom and Bob worked until 5 and got home around 530. That left me alone with my brother after school. I got punched, kicked, pinned down, and told how stupid and worthless I was on a daily basis. At one point he cornered me in the kitchen, and I knew I was about to get my butt kicked, so I pulled out a knife from the block set on the counter and told him I was going to stab him if he came close enough. I was so hurt and so scared at that point I might have done it. He laughed at me and left the kitchen. I stayed there for 30 minutes and finally came out. He was hiding around the corner and pushed me down and beat the crap out of me. Some days after school I would just go home and hide in my closet.

For two years, I was planning my death. I thought about jumping from the balcony, but we were only two stories up. My step dad had a loaded gun in his nightstand next to the porn magazines. I put that gun to my head at least a half a dozen times, but I couldn't pull the trigger because I didn't want my mom to be the one to find me, and she was always the first one home. I thought about hanging myself from the shower with rope, but I didn't know how to tie a knot strong enough. One day when I was 13, my mom was staying home from work. I didn't want to go to school because the head girl of the "popular clique" started calling me names in the hall because her boyfriend broke up with her and he started talking to me. When I asked my mom if I could stay home, she said, "no, go make your bed and go to school." I begged, and she still said, "No!" I said some smart comment to her, and she pushed me backward into the chair and held both my arms so tightly while she yelled in my face. That was my last straw. I went to my room, made my bed and then went to the bathroom, locked the door and swallowed an entire bottle of Tylenol. I walked out, went to the front door and opened it. I almost had it closed behind me, and my mom called my name. When I didn't answer, she opened the door and said, "don't leave like this." I said, "just let me go." She said, "no, I don't want you to go to school like this" and she gave me a hug and said she was sorry. I started crying and couldn't stop and through the sobbing, I told her what I did. I got taken to the emergency room, and the rest is a little of a blur but I remember them giving me ipecac, and it made me throw up so much that it burst the blood vessels in both eyes, my face, neck, and chest. My mom says they pumped my stomach, but I don't remember. That ended up being the best decision I had ever made.

Right after that, they shipped me off to live with my grandparents in Missouri. It was a relief; I was safe. I did sleep walk out their front door and throughout the house. My Grandma used to wake me up on the couch; I was clueless how I got there. I started the 9th grade. It was a good year, and I was blessed with a best friend. While I was too ashamed to tell her what happened to me: she loved me, and I loved her. She gave me the amazing gift of her friendship when I needed it the most. We are still friends to this day.

At the end of the school year, I was flown back to Germany to rejoin my mom, Bob and brother for the 10th grade. Luckily me trying to kill myself freaked my step dad out so much that he never laid a hand on me again. My brother still punched me now and then and still pinned me to the ground to spit on me or to sit on me. Mostly he just made fun of me and told me how stupid I was. Shortly after being back, my mom and Bob were driving me home from a friend's house, my mom turned around from the front seat, and she said, "I know some things happened between you and Bob, but you can't tell anyone, or he will go to jail." I just nodded and that was the end of that. At the end of that year, my brother graduated and went to college.

My mom, Bob and I moved to Indiana where I stayed for 11th and 12th grades. I made some great friends. It was a fun two years. At the same time as my graduation, Bob retired from the Air Force, and we moved to Texas where I started college at 17.

I dated a little in college. I got my heartbroken and broke a few others. I met Rich in college; he was in a fraternity I went to parties at. He asked me out and I didn't really find him attractive but he was fun. His dad made him move to Florida because he was goofing off in school. We visited here and there and kept in touch. After a year, he moved back to be with me and continue college. We dated for the year, he cheated on me and lied about it. I knew he did it, but I chose to believe him and a year later his dad made him move back to Florida again. This time he put a ring on my finger and asked me to go; I did. We were engaged for 4 years, and I kept asking myself if this was enough for me and I couldn't answer it. After six years being together, I decided just to get married; I was 24. It wasn't a good relationship. We didn't have a good intimate connection, and we didn't have any common interests or hobbies. I decided to go back to school and finish my bachelor's degree. I started taking night classes because I worked full time. He continuously told me it was a waste of time, after all, he spent five years in college and never graduated, and he had a job he hated. In 1996 I got pregnant, and in 1997 while still pregnant, I graduated with a Bachelor's of Science degree in Organizational Management.

In August of the same year, the love of my life was born, my daughter. I had never known love like that before. Before she was one, I had told my husband I want to separate, and I moved into the guest room. Up to that point, I paid all the bills and managed our money and accounts. He said he didn't trust me anymore and wanted to do it, so I let him. We had a few confrontations here and there, but mostly I just tried to avoid him. After a year of being separated, he walked into the house and dropped his keys on the floor and said, "the mortgage hasn't been paid, and the house is going to be foreclosed, I'm leaving my car in the driveway, my dad bought me a new one, all the credit card bills are all on you. I'm going bankrupt." Of course, both cars, all the bills and everything else was in my name because he had credit issues and up to that point I had perfect credit. I was forced to file bankruptcy too.

I moved into a small two-bedroom townhome in a not so great area. It was the first time I ever lived on my own (with my daughter too). Occasionally I had to borrow money from a friend to pay my electric, but mostly I made it work. I worked hard and before long moved up within my company. I worked in the education department as an associate producer where I tried to quit 3 times. But they always talked me into staying. The fourth time I tried to quit, they offered me a media manager position handling all the advertising. I accepted and I loved that job. I did it well for 3 years. During that time I bought a house for us in a good neighborhood and it was truly a happy home. It was full of laughter, love, and learning. I got to experience the childhood I never had. We were both kids and loved to giggle, cuddle and have fun together.

Soon, my boss decided to start a new production company, and he asked me to go with him and be a continuity manager. Two other employees came with us. My boss was supposed to do all the training and manage the production staff. I was to make sure the sales team had enough files and help them with story lines and do the advertising. It turns out he did nothing; I had to do it all. I ended up not only closing every contract that company received, I learned the other parts of the business as well because they were being neglected. My boss started creating outrageous bonuses for me so I would be driven to close more contracts. One month the bonus was $10,000 for a certain amount of contracts; that number was almost impossible to hit. I didn't reach it, not even close. After a few months of that, he realized money doesn't motivate me, so he took me to a high-end jewelry store and had them line up the watches that were $10,000 and said pick one. I did, it was a gorgeous Patek Philip watch with diamonds. He said that would be my bonus if I hit the outrageous sales target at the end of the month. He picked something I would not spend my money on but that I loved because it was so beautiful. The next day I printed out a picture of the watch. I cut it out and taped it over my Citizen watch on my arm. Every day that I came to work, I taped it back over my watch while I worked. By the end of the month, that watch was on my arm for real! I was so proud because I had accomplished the impossible. But my boss didn't stop there. I learned to drive on the autobahn growing up and he knew I loved cars. The next bonus was a car allowance for a BMW 650 convertible. He made my quarterly bonus target so high it seemed unreachable. I printed out the picture of the car and had it taped to the side of my computer. Guess what was in my garage at the end of the quarter. There were many other fun bonuses like furniture, private school for my daughter and a membership to the prestigious Harbor Beach Club.

One day, while on my way to the dealership for maintenance a BMW M6 (my 650 on steroids) pulled up next to me. Not only was it a beautiful piece of art, but it was a 500 horsepower piece of art. It was love at first sight, and I said with conviction, "that is my next car!" My car had been in for service a few times, and the manager came over and apologized for the problems. I said jokingly, "can't you just keep my car and give me an M6?" The next day when I went to pick up my car from the service department, the manager came up to me and said, "You've been so nice, I got permission to let you out of your lease so you can get the new M6." In one week's time after declaring it was my next car, I was in it!

Life was good, I was happy. Not because of the things, even though I enjoyed them. I was happy because of my accomplishments and a house full of love. I went a lot of parties at my best friend's brother's house. He bought an amazing house and totally remodeled it. I was completely in love with it. This house was worth close to $2 million dollars, so it was a big "someday" dream for me. Since I believe in vision boards, I got a picture of the house and taped it to my credenza at work. I saw it every day and would imagine what it would be like to live there. If only I could get there, I would have made it! Two years later, in 2008 my friend's brother moved their family business to Georgia, and they put the house up for sale for $1.4 million because the market had dropped. It was on the market for a year when I went to Vegas with my friend for a convention, and her brother was there too. I asked him how my house was and he replied that they had an offer for $875,000 on a short sale, but they were waiting on the bank to see if it would go through. I was shocked. I knew the market had crashed but that price was a steal! The bank took too long and the buyer backed out, so I knew I had to do something. My mom and I put an offer in. After about a month of pins and needles with no answer, I asked the owner for permission to speak to his bank directly, and he allowed it. I spoke to the bank rep, and she explained how slow the process was and that she was responsible for over 200 files at the same time. I called her every few days, and I had established a great rapport. About a month after that, our offer got rejected. When I called her back, she explained that person who reviewed the offer wasn't the one she hoped for, so I asked her if she would resubmit the offer to the "right" one for me. The resubmission process took 2 months and again we got rejected. She told me it already had a foreclosure date and it was cheaper for them to foreclose on it than to accept the offer. I was heartbroken. Right before the foreclosure day, I wrote a letter saying I know these files are numbers to the bank but I just want you to know who this number is and what this house would mean to us. I wrote that I was a single mom and my mom was widow that lived in Texas and this house would allow us to have a place together. I attached a picture of the 3 of us. I called the representative at the bank and asked her if she would please present it just one more time. She said she would. I got a call a day later saying they accepted it. I just got my dream house! The exact house that was posted on my vision board on my credenza for two years! I had made it!

Shortly after that, I started a TV production company and left my old boss behind. I lived in that house for 6 and half years until my daughter went to college. The house was almost 5,000 square feet and felt so empty without her. Just recently, I sold it for a nice profit and moved into a cute, cozy house across the street from the beach.

What I learned in the process:

What you focus on you bring about. That works for the good and the bad. If you expect something is going to be a certain way, chances are it will. You can live in the past or you can live for today. Forgiveness does not change the past but it does enlarge the future.

It took me getting my dream cars, dream house, and dream life to realize external things can never make you sustainably happy or give you self-worth. Happiness is a state of mind that you choose every day. Self-worth comes from loving yourself.

The people and situations that you dislike, maybe even hate and resent just might be the things that are pushing you forward. If my boss had kept his word about training and doing his job, I would never have had to learn how to run a production company.

My brother ended up being a rocket scientist and a doctor. He got his master's degree from MIT in aeronautical and astronautical engineering and became an F-16 pilot. When he got bored with that, he quit and went to Johns Hopkins and became a doctor. I had a good trainer for life

210

experiences. While he was a sparring partner for sure, one that was stronger and smarter than me, I learned how to compete. It pushed me to need to be better. I tried harder and learned quickly how to succeed in every job that I ever had because I had something to prove. It's because of him that I was given the gift of competition and it has served me well in business.

My mom gave me a gift too. I learned to be an amazing mother to my daughter because I knew what it looked and felt like to be dismissed. I'm so blessed to have the relationship I have with my 19-year-old smart, loving, compassionate and beautiful daughter. I got to relive my childhood with her. I was single for the first 13 years of her life, and we were two giggly, playful and loving girls. My mom made me into that mother, and I'm grateful.

My stepdad gave me the gift of compassion and empathy. My heart is huge and tender for all people, especially those suffering. I got my vivid imagination from escaping all of those horrible events. I could take myself anywhere in my mind and feel as if I was actually there. I can still do that. It has served me well in my television production career.

Every time my heart gets sliced open, and with every scar that comes from stitching it back up, it just gets more beautiful and more loving. Sometimes the stitching takes longer, but usually, the lessons learned are that much more meaningful. Just like a butterfly in a cocoon, it comes out when it's ready and is no longer a caterpillar; it has beautiful wings.

"Love harder than any pain you've ever felt."
Author Unknown

*"Experience is a brutal teacher, but you learn.
My God, do you learn."*
C.S. Lewis

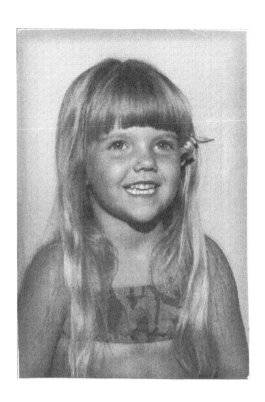

Marie Kiana is the Executive Producer and owner of a television production company and media company that produces and distributes national television shows. She has been in the television business for 20 years and holds a Bachelor of Science in Organizational Management but believes most education comes from life.

Kiana has lived in Hawaii, California, Spain, Germany, Missouri, Indiana, and Texas growing up and has called Florida home for the last twenty-five years. She has been on a journey of a lifetime learning to embrace the child inside.

14

The Battle Within

Tracy Baumer

I'm just like the girl that is portrayed by Meg Ryan in the movie "You've Got Mail." The kind who never has a "zinger" when someone is mean or making statements that aren't true. The one who walks away thinking about what they should have said and regrets not defending herself. I lie awake at night thinking about it and getting prepared for the next time it happens. Only, I am still never prepared! In the moment, when someone is being mean, it's almost like I am stunned into silence. Okay, so maybe once or twice I have snapped back with biting words, and I had the same reaction as in the movie- it doesn't feel good. So, does that make me a pushover? I used to think so. I used to think that it was clever to snap back. Then time and experience taught me that I must stay true to who I am and not worry about being like other people. I have found that resiliency is not about fighting back, it's about fighting within!

If it's not "us" against "them" and we are truly just fighting an internal battle, then what does it mean to be resilient and how do we know if we are? I can tell you right now that you have what it takes to survive anything that happens in life! And, in fact, none of us really have obstacles to overcome and barriers to face. Instead, we have choices and decisions to make. Sometimes, the choices offered aren't any that we like or had planned for, but they are choices nonetheless. I can choose to let a new, unplanned circumstance affect me negatively, or I can choose to see it as an opportunity. This might sound Pollyanna-ish, but we need to listen to our inside voice. The inside voice is built from your values and grows over time. We form certain beliefs and marry that with our innate talents to form a very strong muscle called "resiliency." Your inside voice will tell you when something is wrong and it will guide you toward ways of overcoming the challenges you perceive. Your way of handling life is probably different than mine and that of your friend's, and that's okay. You are the one who must live with your choices, so own them. Only you can decide what to do in each situation. Our true struggles come from inconsistencies in decisions we make and what we believe in. You become resilient by learning to make, and live with, decisions.

The good news is that you have opportunities to build up your resiliency muscle every day! We all have things that get in our way or make us change our path. These smaller decisions are what help you acquire resiliency muscle memory for when the larger opportunities arise. Think about it, I bet just yesterday you got stuck in traffic or ran into a tough co-worker, family member, or friend. Maybe you couldn't find the perfect outfit for that special event or worse, it rained and ruined your brand-new shoes! These are all examples of opportunities to learn adaptability and resiliency. These examples may seem petty but I challenge you to think of these little moments as "practice" for what is yet to come. We need to start taking credit for all the small victories that occur each day. From them, you become confident knowing you will be prepared to perform later.

What happens when the big one comes? How will I perform when a true traumatic event happens in my life? I don't know yet because I have only had small to medium trials in my life. When I was young, we moved out of state and far away from grandparents, cousins, and friends. We are a big Italian family and I am a sentimental fool, so it was impactful! My parents divorced in High School; another impactful situation. I had a choice to feel sorry for myself or make the most of the situation. I hadn't taken personality tests or read books about different styles and approaches at that time. I was unable to weigh pros and cons and over think my process, instead I acted gutturally. I responded in my most natural way. I talked to anyone who would listen! Turns out, that's what works for me- it's scientifically proven beyond just my own personal experience. I am the personality type who gains energy from external resources, which in my case is in the form of talking through situations with others. As a kid, I didn't know any other way and I didn't take the time to think about it, I just acted. Now as an adult, I make time to talk through my situations... with anyone who will listen. My two pets could tell you a lot of stories! I know I can get through any big, traumatic event because I have been practicing my resiliency for a very long time! My advice is for you to solve things using your natural talents and in the manner that capitalizes on your natural strengths.

Sure, there are some people who are be labeled as resilient. These are the folks that are spoken about in news stories or at lunch tables. They have had huge traumas in their life and came out on top. I admire them and am inspired by their stories. But, don't we all have odds to overcome? My point is that we all have obstacles (sometimes every day). I am guessing that the people who overcome extreme odds learned to do so before they got into those extreme circumstances. They made the choice to find a way of making it all work. It isn't because they are super human, it's because they practice resiliency daily and own their choices. Resilient people accept the power they have within.

I love history. We can learn so much by looking back and reflecting. I did not major in this subject or take many formal courses on history, but I love it; it's my hobby. History can be yesterday or ten thousand years ago. Tidbits of the past help explain why things are the way they are now. This is also a strategy for overcoming your obstacles. For example, if I look back on the last 7 years of historical data regarding my commute to work, I know that most residents on my end of town get on the road between 7:00 and 7:40 in the morning. Therefore, I leave at 6:45 to "beat the traffic." There are some mornings that the closet picks a fight, and I lose! On these days, I lean on my survival kit of gum (for blowing bubbles to entertain myself), the radio (to experience many mood swings from happiness to sadness, depending on the song), and my phone (to make needed phone calls- hands-free of course!). I am resilient to the stress of traffic! Again, I believe resiliency is a choice that comes from within. I choose to not let traffic change my mood. I use history to help me learn and adapt to the needs of today. Now, if the traffic is due to rain, I lose my mind! I mean, c'mon people, it's just water! But, for the most part, traffic is something that helps me flex my resiliency muscle.

History has proven that we are a resilient species. We make the decision to either accept our circumstances or move into action to change things.

When making the decision to accept or change, we should listen to our inside voice while also seeking input from exterior resources. This can be people or things. I love looking to nature for answers and inspiration. Birds fly south in the winter. Animals in the Serengeti move with the waxing and waning water. I know that I am not the only one who looks to nature for ideas because many country songs have been written about trees bending to avoid breaking. So, why do we as humans, forget to bend? I don't have the answer, but maybe it has something to do with our fears and egos. These two darn things get in the way of a lot of great decisions! Look back in history at either large scale events or even your own past. We all have done things and made decisions that can be lessons for today.

High School- UGH! The things we did and the decisions we made because of fear and ego…. I apologize for making you think of your high school years, so I will go back to country music. What do some of the other country songs sing about? They sing about men and women being the same no matter the age of the person. Heck, I believe that amusement parks are successful because we are all kids of many different ages. If this is the case, then learning to be resilient for every small event along the way will help you later in life when the larger events occur.

Take inventory and define yourself. There are tons of ways to do this and I love a good personality test! I have some favorites, but there are many different types of tests because we are all different. Try a bunch of them and follow the one(s) that speak most to you. I recommend this because, no matter who you are and how intelligent you are, it's difficult to analyze yourself. I have been fortunate enough to work for companies who have sponsored this type feedback in many forms. I have experienced over two dozen forms of coaching by way of personality assessments, peer reviews, and leadership feedback. These resources have helped me learn who I am and how to harness that power to do the things I enjoy doing.

My solace comes from talking through situations. I am thankful that I had the opportunity to learn this about myself and how to harness my natural talents. I get energy and inspiration from meeting people and learning new perspectives. Therefore, I listen to others and specifically, to how they have overcome large obstacles or disasters. I enjoy all the beauty found in nature. From this beauty, we can learn many strategies for becoming resilient. Historical events, both our own personal stories and large-scale, global events teach us what to do and what to avoid. It also teaches us that we learn to become resilient one step at a time. The people I know who have recovered, and even thrive, after terrible situations, chose to take the first step and committed to taking all additional steps. It's a journey and we are all in it together every day.

I have had my fair share of disappointments and challenges in life, both professionally and personally. I choose to harness my natural abilities, stay my course and address each challenge as it comes in hopes that I am learning to overcome any big challenge that might come my way. And, yes, Meg Ryan's character ends up overcoming her obstacles and gets a great guy and tons of money.... I didn't say we all live a Hollywood dream, but I do believe in you. Just when you think you are done and can't go on any longer, remember your power within and take the next step.

Tracy Baumer is married with two children. She is a Human Resources professional and has always believed that being a leader at work helps you become a better parent and vice versa. A life-long learner, Tracy asks questions and does not turn down the opportunity to try new things; this is her first attempt at professional writing. She encourages everyone to take calculated risks and listen to nature.

44371923R00129

Made in the USA
Middletown, DE
04 June 2017